Ghostly Towers

*The exciting adventure game that will
really give you the creeps!*

Stephen Thraves

Illustrated by Peter Dennis

HODDER AND STOUGHTON
LONDON SYDNEY AUCKLAND

British Library Cataloguing in Publication Data

Thraves, Stephen
 Ghostly towers.
 I. Title   II. Series
 823.914[F]

 ISBN 0-340-53285-8

First published 1990
Fourth impression 1992

Published by Hodder and Stoughton Children's Books,
a division of Hodder and Stoughton Ltd,
Mill Road, Dunton Green, Sevenoaks, Kent TN13 2YA

Photoset by Rowland Phototypesetting Ltd,
Bury St Edmunds, Suffolk

Printed in Great Britain by
BPCC Hazells Ltd
Member of BPCC Ltd

Dare you explore GHOSTLY TOWERS? Its real name is Oastley Towers, one-time residence of Sir Edward Oastley, but there have been so many strange sightings at the derelict estate that the petrified locals have renamed it. First there was the headless figure near the gates, then the luminous apparition at one of the windows, then the white lady drifting across the lake . . .

With all these scary goings-on, you might wonder why you should *want* to explore GHOSTLY TOWERS. Surely, any sensible person would keep well away from the eerie place! But you've heard rumours that a priceless diamond necklace is hidden somewhere on the gloomy estate. It was the possession of Sir Edward's beautiful wife, Rowena, and is said to be the finest piece of jewellery ever to grace a female neck.

You will not necessarily uncover the diamonds on your first exploration. It may well take several goes. Keep trying, though, and you will eventually be successful.

Even when you *have* found the diamonds, you may want to try further explorations. Because some people say that there is more than one diamond necklace hidden in GHOSTLY TOWERS; indeed, as many as three! And there are many different routes you can take through the house and grounds – each route involving different clues and adventures.

So the game can be played over and over again, as many times as your nerves can stand it!

PREPARATION FOR YOUR VISIT

Well, you've certainly no intention of exploring Ghostly Towers alone! You'd like some company on this spine-chilling mission. So you pay a call on Professor Bones, the celebrated 'ghostologist'. A thin, absent-minded little man, he is fascinated by your account of Ghostly Towers and says he would be delighted to join your exploration.

Equally enthusiastic is the other ghost expert you invite; Miss Harriet Crumble, the famous medium. She says she'll bring along her *spirit dice*, which is a sort of portable 'crystal ball' to help make important decisions. Rather less enthusiastic, however, is her Scottish terrier, Spooks. The more the eccentric Miss Crumble warms to your idea of exploring Ghostly Towers, the more Spooks's little white body shakes! He knows he could never let his mistress down, but he often wishes he had a more normal owner. One who went to feed the ducks, for instance, or just knitted quietly all day. Yes, that would be rather nice . . .

Having organised your exploration party, you now pay a visit on Smith, Twitch and Creak, the company of lawyers who used to represent the Oastley Towers Estate. You've never seen such a dusty office! The only one in the company now is a very doddery Mr Cecil Creak, the original Creak's great, great grandson.

You ask Mr Creak if he can give you any information about Ghostly Towers that may help your exploration. He finally manages to produce a crumbling folder. This contains a plan of Oastley Towers, two rusty keys (one red, one blue), and a copy of Sir Edward's will. The keys, you're sure, are to certain rooms in Ghostly Towers, but the will is a rather more curious item. It's not like a normal will with lots of boring, muddled sentences, but it's a series of little drawings. Next to each drawing are what appear to be clues!

Anyway, Mr Creak is happy to let you have these various items, and so you take the folder with you. As you're walking away from his office, however, he comes rushing up to you, panting, and with an anxious look on his face. He's just found a scrap of paper on his office floor. It must have fallen out of the folder. In faded, spidery handwriting, it warns that any person starting out in search of the diamonds with more than *one* of the items, will be cursed for ever!

That's all the preparation complete. You're now ready to begin your adventure . . .

WHAT TO DO

Your exploration of Ghostly Towers starts at PARAGRAPH ONE. At the end of that paragraph, you will be instructed to go to another paragraph. You keep following these instructions until – hopefully – you uncover the hidden diamonds.

Quite often during the exploration, you will need one of the ITEMS given to you by Mr Creak – those were the will, the red key, the blue key, and the plan of the estate. These ITEMS accompany this book but, because of that terrible curse, you daren't start out with any more than *one* of them. So decide which of the four ITEMS is likely to be the most useful. Be very careful in making this choice because some ITEMS offer you a better chance of completing the adventure than others. Place the ITEM you have chosen into the slit of the FOLDER CARD.

You may well discover other ITEMS during your exploration of the house and its grounds. If you do, these can be added to the one you set out with – and so, when instructed, place these extra ITEMS into the slit of the FOLDER CARD as well. The purpose of this card is to tell you exactly which ITEMS you have for use at any one time (so, after an ITEM has helped at a particular paragraph, always remember to return it to your FOLDER CARD). Any ITEM not contained in this card **cannot be used or consulted**, and therefore should be kept out of play.

I think I ought to point out that there's more than a fair chance of seeing ghosts during your exploration of the house and its grounds. I don't like having to say this, but I feel it's only right to warn you. And they're also rather mean ghosts, tending to appear on those occasions when you've just found that you don't have the appropriate ITEM with you.

If you *do* see a ghost, you must, as soon as you've recovered from the shock, record it on the GHOST COUNTER included in the wallet. This is a special invention of Professor Bones for adding up hauntings. You begin your adventure with the GHOST COUNTER set at *zero* – so rotate the disc until **0** appears in the window. Every time you experience a 'haunting', you turn the disc **clockwise** until the next number appears. Your nerves can stand one haunting . . . two . . . even three, but when the GHOST COUNTER shows you've had *four* hauntings, you must immediately leave Ghostly Towers, stopping the game there. Of course, you can always make another exploration (perhaps setting out with a different ITEM this time to see if it gives you more luck), but you can only do this by starting at **paragraph one** again.

I'm not sure how wise you are venturing into Ghostly Towers but if you must continue, turn the page. And I wish you luck! I've a horrible feeling you may need it . . .

1

Your heart sinks as your little group approaches the massive gates of Ghostly Towers. You'd assumed that the Professor and Miss Crumble would be more used to this sort of thing, able to give you reassurance. But they're as white as you are! And as for poor little Spooks, he's trembling from nose to tail! 'The place is a lot eerier than I was expecting,' the Professor whispers after a gulp. 'And there's still a little light in the sky. Goodness knows what it will look like in an hour or so!' You're expecting him to put a hand to the large iron ring on the gates to see if they'll open, but he holds back for someone else to do it. The problem is, you and Miss Crumble are holding back as well! 'I know what we'll do,' Miss Crumble eventually suggests. 'We'll let the spirits decide who's to try the gates. I'll consult my dice!'

Throw the SPIRIT DICE – then turn to the appropriate paragraph number.

If ☠ thrown   go to 300

If 🦇 thrown   go to 135

If 👻 thrown   go to 71

2

Your little group quickly leaves the footbridge and the lake and ventures deeper into the shadowy grounds. But Miss Crumble won't stop talking about it. 'With all those reeds at the edge, it very much reminds me of the lake at Berkley Manor,' she informs you cheerfully. 'The lady of the house drowned right in the middle, poor dear. They say her weeping figure can sometimes be seen drifting . . .' You suddenly interrupt her, however, really not desiring any more of this story. Your nerves are bad enough as it is! 'Why don't we check the footbridge's position on the plan of the estate?' you suggest quickly.

If you have the ESTATE PLAN in your FOLDER, use it to find which square the footbridge is in – then follow the instruction below. If you don't, you'll have to guess which instruction to follow.

If you think A2	go to 45
If you think A3	go to 184
If you think B3	go to 311

3

You're just about to continue your walk up the driveway when Miss Crumble points out a long-overgrown hedge a few hundred metres to your right. 'I do believe it's a maze!' she exclaims. 'How enchanting! And what a wonderful hiding place for the diamonds it would be!' You and Professor Bones are inclined to agree with her and so you decide to leave the driveway for a while in order to investigate the maze. When you reach its entrance, however, you find that it is barred by a tall iron gate. 'What a nuisance!' Miss Crumble tuts on discovering that the gate is firmly locked. 'I wonder if one of those two keys would help?'

Do you have either of the KEYS in your FOLDER? If you do,

place it exactly over the gate's 'lock' below to see whether it works – then follow the instruction. (You may try both keys if you have them.) If you don't have either of the KEYS – or your KEY doesn't work – go to 42 instead.

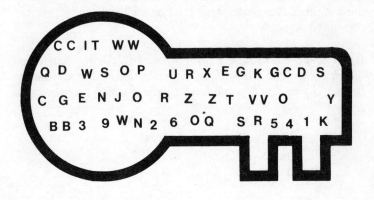

4

'Spooks!' Miss Crumble cries with joy as her little dog appears round the hedge. 'The panting was you! How did you get behind us all when you were in front before?' The answer is quite simple. You're all well and truly lost in the maze, just going round in circles! 'Maybe it's a sort of trick maze,' the Professor comments as you grow more and more desperate, turning this way and that, 'where there's a route in but not out. I'm reminded of some cliff steps in Cornwall, said to have been cut by the Devil. They're never the same number counting down as counting up!' You're just about to tell the Professor that that sort of story doesn't help at all at the present moment, when you suddenly reach the outside of the maze. Phew! *Go to 122.*

5

The fir trees seem to grow darker and darker, noisier and noisier. It's difficult to believe that even the inside of the mansion will be as spooky as this! As you're walking along, feeling very anxious,

Spooks suddenly starts to sniff at some of the fallen pine-cones. Has he picked up the scent of a ghost, you wonder nervously, or don't ghosts have scents? 'A very interesting question!' Professor Bones replies when you ask him about it. 'In most cases they don't. But I heard of one ghost – a lady in white – who would leave a strong perfume wherever she drifted.' You're just beginning to worry about this, wishing that the Professor hadn't told you, when you realise that Spooks hasn't picked up the scent of a ghost. He has picked up *something*, though. A large blue key!

If you don't already have it there, put the BLUE KEY into your FOLDER. Now go to 20.

6

Your first haunting! When you have recovered from the shock, record it on your GHOST COUNTER. Now go to 65.

7

But it proves not to be a spirit at all – right sort or otherwise! For a large hare suddenly appears from where you had heard the noise, its startled eyes staring at you for a moment. Then it hops away over the crackly fallen leaves. 'Was that your spirit, Miss Crumble?' the Professor can't resist asking her with a bit of a smile. 'It looked just like a hare to me!' Miss Crumble gives an irritated tut. 'Now you've broken my trance, Professor,' she accuses him. 'No, of course it wasn't my spirit. Now, how are we going to work out how to unlock the bucket?' But you tell her that you no longer have to. You've just given the bucket a good shake and there's not the slightest rattling sound from inside. It's obviously empty! *Go to 207.*

8

You suddenly remember that you didn't bring the estate plan with you, however. Your bad memory just shows how nervous you're becoming! The nerves are because you know that very soon now the mansion itself is going to loom out of the darkness ahead. It happens sooner than you're expecting. 'Good grief!' Miss Crumble exclaims, taking several steps back as the huge turreted silhouette suddenly appears not far in front of you. 'It's the spookiest place I've ever laid eyes on!' You and Professor Bones take even more steps back, your gaze riveted to the tower on the left. You're certain you saw something move in the topmost window. You anxiously wait to see if it happens again . . . *Go to 38.*

9

'Who has the dice chosen, Miss Crumble?' you ask anxiously as she studies how it has landed. 'It's not me, is it?' She shakes her head. 'No, I'm afraid it's you, Professor,' she answers. So Professor Bones nervously leads you all towards the stables, gradually approaching the cobbled yard. 'That's strange,' he remarks, 'we could hear one of the stable doors banging a few minutes ago, but now every one appears to be locked!' He walks right up to one of them to check. 'Yes, it's firmly locked all right,' he says, mystified. 'Look, there's a massive padlock on it. Perhaps one of those two keys will fit?'

Do you have either of the KEYS in your FOLDER? If you do, place it exactly over the stable door's 'lock' below to see whether it works – then follow the instruction. (You may try both KEYS if you have them.) If you don't have either of the KEYS – or your KEY doesn't work – go to 242 instead.

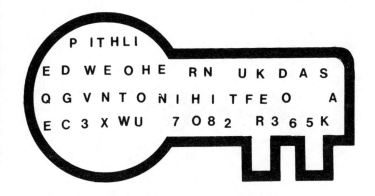

10

Miss Crumble is determined to have her way over finding Sir Edward's gravestone, however. 'I'm sure if I stand next to it, Sir Edward will try and get in touch with me,' she insists eagerly. 'I shan't be a minute!' She cheerfully flits from one gravestone to another, peering down at their inscriptions. 'Here it is!' she suddenly calls back with delight. 'Now I'll just close my eyes and wait for Sir Edward to send me a message. He might even tell me exactly where the diamonds are!' You certainly can't criticise Miss Crumble's degree of effort – she closes her eyes as tightly as they will go, wrinkling her whole face – but it's all to no avail. Perhaps Sir Edward just isn't very sociable this evening! *Go to 270.*

Sir Edward's clue tells you that the diamonds are definitely hidden somewhere *inside* the house. You're not sure whether this is good news or bad! On the one hand it means that you don't have to search the entire grounds any more. But on the other, it means that you can't get out of entering that spooky mansion! It wouldn't be so bad if you had more confidence in your two 'specialist' companions. You'd originally thought they would be the ideal people to take along with you on this exploration. But they seem just as scared of ghosts as you are. In fact, you wonder whether Professor Bones has ever actually seen one before! And as for Miss Crumble, the famous medium . . . you've a horrible suspicion that she's just a charming fraud! *Go to 140.*

When you have recovered from this haunting, record it on the GHOST COUNTER. Now go to 122.

'You might as well keep the candle, Professor Bones,' Miss Crumble tells him. 'My spirit dice has again chosen *you* to take the lead!' The Professor has only carried the candle a few steps, however, when he suddenly stops. 'W-w-what's that?' he asks, his thin body shaking. 'Can you see? Further down the hall? It's someone dressed in white, isn't it?' You and Miss Crumble anxiously peer in the direction the Professor's trembling finger is pointing. 'No, it's not someone dressed in white, Professor,' you chuckle with relief. 'It just looks white because of the reflection of your candle. They're actually dressed in silver. It's merely a suit of armour standing there!' *Go to 325.*

14

When you have recovered from this haunting, record it on your GHOST COUNTER. Now go to 101.

15

You've now been in the chapel for a good twenty minutes and you decide that you had better start moving again before it gets completely dark outside. While you and Professor Bones are warily checking at the door to make sure there are no ghosts around, Miss Crumble suddenly takes an interest in two crossed flags displayed on the chapel wall. They are very old and the designs on them are so faded that they're hardly distinguishable. But they're just visible enough to make Miss Crumble wonder if one of Sir Edward's clues is hidden there!

Do you have Sir Edward's WILL in your FOLDER? If you do, check whether any part of the flags' designs is included there – then follow the appropriate instruction to find out his clue. If not, go to 94 instead.

16

'But since we didn't bring Sir Edward's will with us,' the Professor adds with a disappointed grimace, 'we can't know if there's a clue hidden in the drawings.' You therefore suggest leaving the summerhouse. It feels much colder in there than outside. 'Yes, that's odd, isn't it?' Miss Crumble comments as you close the glass door behind you and start to walk away. 'Of course, you know what an icy coldness like that usually means? It means there's some sort of spirit in there!' You really wish Miss Crumble wouldn't unsettle your

nerves like this. In fact she's unsettled them so much that you decide
to turn round to take one last look at the summer-house before it
disappears into the darkness. Of course there weren't any spirits in
there . . . *Go to 281.*

17

Some eight hundred metres further up the driveway from the
statue, you come across an ornate garden seat. 'I bet this is where Sir
Edward and his beloved Rowena would sit and watch the carriages
go by,' Miss Crumble says dreamily. 'I can just see them now; hand
in hand, hopelessly in love!' Well, you hope Miss Crumble can't see
them *too* vividly. You don't want their ghosts suddenly to appear!
'Let's have a little sit-down, shall we?' Miss Crumble suggests. 'So
we can rest our feet. While we're resting, we can locate this seat on
the plan of the estate. It will show us exactly how far we are along the
driveway.'

*Do you have the ESTATE PLAN in your FOLDER? If you do,
use it to find which square the garden seat is in – then follow the
appropriate instruction. If you don't, you'll have to guess which
instruction to follow.*

If you think C3	go to 308
If you think D2	go to 90
If you think D3	go to 136

18

You remind Miss Crumble that you didn't bring Sir Edward's will
with you, and so there's no way of checking whether the gravestone
bears one of his clues. 'Oh well, I'm sure it doesn't!' Miss Crumble
says. 'A man like Sir Edward would hardly go round defacing one of
his own ancestors' tombs.' You're not so sure, though. It sounds
exactly the sort of thing Sir Edward would do! Your little group now
leaves the graveyard but you haven't walked far when you suddenly
hear a moaning sound from behind you. Has one of the spirits been

disturbed by your investigation of the tombs? Is it now getting its own back? You all very slowly look back at the graveyard . . . ***Go to 330.***

You're just informing Professor Bones that you didn't bring the estate plan with you when you suddenly notice that Spooks is looking rather strange. His ears are cocked and his entire body has gone completely rigid. 'What's wrong, Spooks?' you ask him anxiously. But then you suddenly hear a noise from further up the driveway. It sounds like an old-fashioned carriage! 'It's probably just a trick of the wind,' the Professor says uncertainly as you all peer into the dark. 'I can't see anything over there!' The noise gradually becomes louder, however. Any moment now, you're sure something horrible is going to appear . . . ***Go to 68.***

A short time later, your little group finds itself approaching a tiny church, hidden away right in the corner of the estate. It stands quiet and abandoned against the darkening sky. Ivy twists out of control up its walls and the wind howls through its broken windows. 'It must be the Oastley family chapel,' Miss Crumble remarks as you all stare at the eerie silhouette. 'Where they had their services and said their prayers.' But was it *also* where the diamonds were hidden, you all wonder. There's only one way to find out . . . and that is to enter the forbidding chapel! Miss Crumble suggests throwing her spirit dice to decide who should step in first . . .

Throw the SPIRIT DICE – then turn to the appropriate number.

If ☠ thrown   go to 255

If 🦇 thrown   go to 167

If 👻 thrown   go to 190

21

It looks as if you did go to all this trouble for nothing, after all! 'Perhaps there's another door somewhere round the house,' Miss Crumble tries to console you all. 'One that isn't locked!' So your little group starts to walk to the right of the front door, and it's only a matter of a few steps, in fact, before you find something. Not a door, but an open sash window. Just as everyone has squeezed through this window into the house, however, it mysteriously slams shut. Was this the work of a ghost lurking outside? You all nervously back away from the window, wondering if something is suddenly going to appear there . . . *Go to 293.*

22

You've left the little glass building some distance behind when Miss Crumble suddenly trips and sprawls to the ground. 'Oh, do stop fussing, you two!' she says as you and the Professor attempt to help her up. 'You'd be of more use having a closer look at this box I tripped over. Unless I'm much mistaken, it's a sort of small treasure chest!' With growing excitement, you and the Professor come to that conclusion too. With its curved lid, it certainly *looks* like a treasure chest! You all realise there's a very good chance the diamonds are inside. But how do you *get* inside? The box is securely locked! Perhaps one of those keys will work . . .

Do you have either of the two KEYS in your FOLDER? If you

do, place it exactly over the box's 'lock' below to see if it works –
then follow the instruction. (You may try both keys if you have
them.) If you don't have either of the KEYS – or your KEY
doesn't work – go to 241 instead.

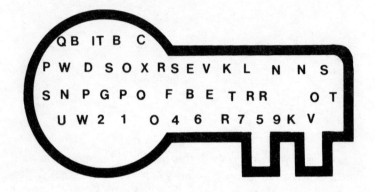

23

You heave open the heavy door as fast as you can, and all rush
outside, making for the nearest large tree. 'No one's emerged,' Miss
Crumble observes after a while, as you all peep from behind the
wide trunk. 'Perhaps the ghost has finished his wanderings for the
evening and has disappeared again. Just trot inside, Spooks, and
check!' But, much to Spooks's relief, you tell Miss Crumble that it
would be unfair to send him back there alone. 'We'll all go!' you
insist, cautiously leading the way to the bottom of the steps again. It
appears that Miss Crumble was right, though. The ghost must have
finished for the evening because the clonking sound has stopped.
Go to 331.

24

After eagerly pushing at the unlocked door, you, Miss Crumble and
Spooks find yourselves staring into a dark passage. 'It must be a
secret route to another part of the house,' you remark as you
cautiously start to follow it. Fortunately, the passage isn't very long
and soon brings you to a second door which you all lean on to try and

open. Suddenly, the door swings round and you find yourselves in . . . the library! You hear a startled gasp from there as you suddenly emerge. It's the Professor! 'Where on earth did you three come from?' he cries. 'This was just a section of bookshelves a moment ago. I couldn't resist going back to them.' As you're explaining to the Professor about the secret passage, Miss Crumble notices that Spooks has a large blue key between his teeth. He must have found it in there.

If you don't already have it, put the BLUE KEY into your FOLDER. Now go to 178.

25

When you have recovered from this haunting, record it on the GHOST COUNTER. Now go to 85.

26

Sir Edward's clue tells you that you've come to the wrong part of the tower for the diamonds! 'What on earth could that mean?' the Professor asks, mystified. 'Surely, there is only one part you *can* go to – the top!' But, unless it was one of his little jokes, Sir Edward presumably knew what he was talking about . . . so you all start to descend the stone steps. You haven't gone very far when Miss Crumble emits a loud scream. 'Something just brushed the side of my face!' she wails. 'We should have closed that door at the top behind us. I'm sure it was a bat!' Rather unsympathetically, the rest of you let out a huge sigh of relief. Was that all . . . a bat? For one terrible moment you thought she might have been talking about a ghost! *Go to 289.*

27

Although you all nearly break your backs in the process, you finally loosen the heavy trap-door. It now slowly creaks open, revealing a short flight of crumbling stone steps. 'There seems to be a sort of dungeon down there,' the Professor remarks, anxiously peering in. 'It must date back to the time when this tower was part of a castle, long before the house was built on to it. I'm afraid we're going to have to explore this dungeon. I'm sure you'll agree that there's a very good chance the diamonds are hidden down there!' Since none of you is at all keen to take the lead down the dark steps, Miss Crumble suggests letting her spirit dice pick someone.

Throw the SPIRIT DICE – then turn to the appropriate number.

If ☠ thrown	go to 53
If 🦇 thrown	go to 256
If 👻 thrown	go to 123

'It's chosen me!' Miss Crumble exclaims softly as she studies her spirit dice. 'But it's not me alone. The spirit dice says that Spooks should join me at the front!' Spooks seems very suspicious about this. He appears to be wondering if the spirit dice really did decide that. But he eventually resigns himself to it, nervously trotting alongside his mistress as she leads the way down the eerie steps. You all finally reach the bottom of the dark stairway and encounter a locked door. 'What's that?' the Professor suddenly cries on hearing a slight rustling noise above. 'It sounds like someone in a long, trailing dress coming down the steps! Quick, we've got to get through this door before she comes any closer! Do we have the right key?'

Do you have either of the KEYS in your FOLDER? If you do, place it exactly over the door's 'lock' below to see whether it works – then follow the instruction. (You may try both KEYS if you have them.) If you don't have either of the KEYS – or your KEY doesn't work – go to 215 instead.

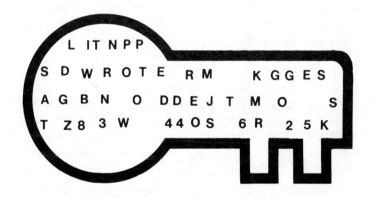

Miss Crumble eagerly pulls out the top drawer and brings the candle to it. 'It's full of beautiful hairbrushes,' she says, lifting one out. 'Look, there are some initials engraved on the back – *R.O.* You know whose they are, don't you? Rowena Oastley's! This must have been *her* room.' You and Professor Bones are much more interested in whether the diamonds are hidden in any of the drawers, though. Spooks too. After all, the sooner the diamonds are found, the sooner he can leave this scary place! But the diamonds aren't in any of the drawers, unfortunately. The lower drawers just contain scent bottles, ribbons and various other personal items that belonged to Lady Rowena. *Go to 199.*

30

Sir Edward's clue tells you that you're unlikely to uncover the diamonds unless you have all four items in your possession: the plan, the will, and the two keys. But don't worry if you don't have them all *yet*, it adds, there are quite a number hidden in the grounds. All you have to do is find them! 'He sounds quite a joker, does Sir Edward,' the Professor remarks with a worried frown. 'That concerns me a little. In my researches, I have found that those with a strong sense of humour always make the most likely ghosts. They can't resist making people jump!' There's something that is beginning to concern you a little as well. You thought the Professor was looking forward to meeting some ghosts, but he seems rather to have changed his mind! *Go to 145.*

31

'Right, here goes!' the Professor says sportingly after Miss Crumble tells him that *he* was the choice of the spirit dice. He uses both hands to grip the handle above the well and it makes a horrible grinding noise as it slowly starts to turn. 'I'm sorry I can't be any quicker,' the

Professor pants, using as much strength as his scrawny body can muster, 'but everything's so rusty.' At last the bucket nears the top, occasionally clanking against the side of the well. Spooks puts his paws over his eyes as the clanks grow louder and louder! 'It's safe to look now, Spooks!' the Professor tells him a few seconds later. 'The bucket's completely empty!' Although you're disappointed, you decide to look for the well on the plan of the estate. You'll at least know exactly where you are!

Use the ESTATE PLAN to find which square the well is in – then follow the appropriate instruction. If you don't have it in your FOLDER, you'll have to guess which instruction to follow.

If you think A2	go to 70
If you think B2	go to 266
If you think B3	go to 91

32

When you have recovered from this haunting, record it on the GHOST COUNTER. Now go to 92.

You very cautiously lift the lid of the box and you all peer inside. The news is both good and bad. The good news is that there *aren't* any remains inside . . . so it's not a coffin! But the bad news is that there isn't anything else inside either. 'I really thought that the diamonds would be in there,' the Professor says sadly as you shut the lid again. 'But we mustn't lose hope. I'm convinced they're in this dungeon somewhere!' You wish that you could be as convinced. You don't think your nerves can stand much more of this awful place. And, by the look of his trembling legs, Spooks seems to be feeling exactly the same! ***Go to 212.***

34

You're all feeling most uneasy about this very top part of the mansion and so you agree to search the nursery as swiftly as possible. 'Perhaps the diamonds are hidden at the bottom of this toy-chest,' the Professor says, eagerly tearing away the cobwebs covering it and rummaging through the contents. But all he can find in there are old building bricks and a little tin music box. He nearly hits the ceiling in shock when it suddenly starts to play! Searching a dusty cupboard in the other corner of the room, Miss Crumble discovers a much bigger box, painted in red and yellow . . . ***Go to 284.***

35

Miss Crumble goes quite pale as she studies her dice. 'It's chosen *me* to enter the mansion first,' she announces quietly. She's just about to put her hand to the iron ring on the door when she notices that the gnarled oak has a date carved into it – *1750*. That's not the only thing carved there. Some strange symbols have also been gouged into the door. 'I wonder if one of these is a clue from Sir Edward?' she asks, delighted at the excuse to delay entering the mansion for a moment. 'Do we have his will with us?'

If you do have his WILL in your FOLDER, check whether any of the symbols shown below are included there – then follow the appropriate instruction to find out his clue. If you don't, go to 124 instead.

36

'Anyone got any other ideas?' you ask, giving the locked gates a disappointed rattle. Spooks's suggestion seems to be to turn round and go home, because he starts delightedly trotting away. But Miss Crumble sternly fetches him back! 'We'll just have to try and climb the gates,' she proposes, much to your surprise. 'And as for you, naughty Spooks, you're small enough to slip through the gates' railings!' *Go to 150.*

37

There's another sound from that same part of the boundary wall, but this time you're quick enough to see what it is. It's just a squirrel, scampering along the top! 'Well, my senses can't always be right,' Miss Crumble explains rather coyly as you all now finally squeeze your way through the massive gates. 'They do make the occasional mistake!' **Go to 217.**

When you have recovered from this haunting, record it on the GHOST COUNTER. (Don't forget: when you have recorded 4 hauntings, you must immediately stop the adventure and start the game all over again.) Now go to 140.

39

Professor Bones lights one of his candles so you can start to explore the mansion. His bony hand is shaking so much that the flame simply won't keep still, flickering to left and right. It makes eerie shadows dance across the flaking walls. Shuffling along the creaking floorboards, you soon find yourselves at the foot of a broad staircase. There are thick cobwebs draped across the banisters. 'This must lead up to the bedrooms on the first floor – ' a loud thunderstorm has suddenly started outside and you can only just hear Miss Crumble's whisper ' – I think we should explore those first. I'll ask my spirit dice to choose which one of us is to lead up the stairway.'

Throw the SPIRIT DICE – then turn to the appropriate number.

If ☠ thrown   go to 76

If 🦇 thrown   go to 261

If 👻 thrown   go to 198

40

'It must have just been the sound of the wind,' the Professor remarks with relief as you look back at the fountain. 'There's certainly no water flowing there now.' Just to make absolutely sure, you return to the pond and examine the stone figure in the middle. It's a maid holding a jug; and it's from this jug, presumably, that the water would flow into the pool beneath. But the pool is completely dry. 'The fountain obviously hasn't worked for years,' the Professor says confidently. 'Look how rusty and clogged up the drainage hole is. What a disappointment! I really thought we were going to encounter our first ghost.' It has to be said, though, that the Professor doesn't *look* that disappointed! ***Go to 3.***

41

You're just about to go and look for Professor Bones when Spooks starts barking at part of the wooden panelling along one wall. 'Look, he's found a secret door!' you exclaim as you and Miss Crumble hurry over to investigate. 'Can you see? There's a cleverly-disguised lock just here. I wonder if that's what one of those keys is for?'

Do you have either of the KEYS in your FOLDER? If you do, place it exactly over the secret door's 'lock' below to see whether

*it works – then follow the instruction. (You may try both KEYS if
you have them.) If you don't have either of the KEYS – or your
KEY doesn't work – go to 174 instead.*

42

You give the gate a good shake just to make sure it really is locked,
and not just rusted tight. Unfortunately, it is! 'We can't even try
climbing it,' you remark disappointedly. 'With all those brambles
growing over the top of the gate's frame, we'd be ripped to shreds.'
So you decide to forget about the maze, just hoping that the
diamonds *aren't* hidden in there. You haven't left it far behind,
however, when you hear a wailing sound from that direction. Was it
just the wind, or does a spirit haunt the middle of the maze? You
nervously look back to see if there's a ghostly head showing above
the hedges . . . *Go to 146.*

43

'Look, it's just a rabbit!' you exclaim to the others. 'A rabbit
hopping over the dead leaves!' You breathe a huge sigh of relief. You
really thought you were going to see a skeleton dancing about there!
'All right, I'll forgive you this time, Spooks,' Miss Crumble tells her
little dog as you start walking again. 'But next time, check that the
bone doesn't belong to anyone. You wouldn't like someone running

away with your arm or leg, would you?' Keeping the bone firmly between his teeth, Spooks gives a little shake of his head. No, he certainly wouldn't! *Go to 20.*

When you have recovered from this haunting, record it on the GHOST COUNTER. Now go to 159.

You're well aware that you don't have the estate plan with you, of course, but your interruption is enough to make Miss Crumble lose her train of thought. 'Now, where was I?' she asks bewilderedly. 'Can either of you remember?' You and the Professor both pretend you can't, however. 'Was it something to do with wanting to enter Spooks for Crufts?' the Professor starts to suggest innocently, but then you're all suddenly stopped in your tracks by what sounds like someone weeping behind you. It's coming from the middle of the lake! Does this one have a ghost too, you wonder, as you all turn nervously to check . . . *Go to 74.*

Leaving the chapel, you notice a small graveyard nearby. 'It must be the Oastley family burial ground,' Miss Crumble says as you stare at all the eerie crosses and tombs. 'Let's see if we can find which tombstone marks Sir Edward's grave!' But you, Professor Bones and Spooks are not so keen on investigating the mist-shrouded stones. You're sure the diamonds aren't going to be hidden there, anyway. It is *sacred* ground, after all. 'Perhaps we should just look it up on the plan of the estate to find out exactly where we are,' you tactfully propose to Miss Crumble. 'It will be completely dark soon – and we've still got a lot of exploring to do!'

Do you have the PLAN in your FOLDER? If you do, use it to find which square the gravestones are in – then follow the appropriate instruction. If you don't, you'll have to guess which instruction to follow.

If you think D3   go to 73
If you think D4   go to 270
If you think E4   go to 10

47

You now start to explore the rooms on the first floor. They smell badly of damp and you're constantly having to clear the cobwebs from your face. 'Aren't they eerie?' you remark as you reach the biggest of the rooms. 'They can't have been used for years and years.' You all follow Miss Crumble's flickering candle towards a large dressing-table by the window. 'Let's see if there is anything hidden in the drawers,' she suggests, resting the candle on the top. But when she tugs at each of the drawers, she finds that they are locked. 'I wonder if one of those keys would fit?' she asks.

Do you have either of the KEYS in your FOLDER? If you do, place it exactly over the top drawer's 'lock' below to see whether it works – then follow the instruction. (You may try both KEYS if you have them.) If you don't have either of the KEYS – or your KEY doesn't work – go to 169 instead.

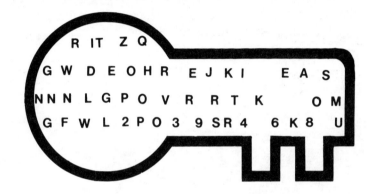

48

The clue in Sir Edward's will tells you to search underneath the seat, being sure to go all the way round. 'Well, we already have done,' Miss Crumble remarks. 'But I suppose there's no harm in doing it again. Perhaps the diamonds are here after all!' So you all get back down on your hands and knees, Spooks helping out with the really cramped bits right at the back. 'Nothing in my section,' you announce after a while. 'How about yours, Miss Crumble?' She gives a disappointed shake of the head. You're expecting the same from the Professor, but his bespectacled face is suddenly quite excited. 'No diamonds,' he says, holding up a large red key, 'but my dusty search wasn't completely in vain!'

If you don't already have it there, put the RED KEY into your FOLDER. Now go to 22.

Checking your folder, however, you remember that you didn't bring Sir Edward's will with you. So there's no way of telling if one of his clues is hidden in the emblem! When your eyes return in disappointment to the tattered flag, you notice something odd about it. You're sure that it has moved down the flagpost slightly! Miss Crumble and the Professor disagree with you, saying it must be your imagination, but then there is no doubt about it. The flag slides right down to the bottom of the post! Either, after all these years, it has coincidentally chosen that very moment to come loose, or someone has lowered it. Someone or some*thing*! Your gazes remain anxiously fixed to the flagpost, waiting to see if anything will suddenly appear there . . . *Go to 152.*

When you have recovered from this haunting, record it on the GHOST COUNTER. Now go to 289.

'Sir Edward's clue says that we should go to the family burial ground,' Miss Crumble excitedly tells you as she consults his will, 'and then find the gravestone for his great aunt Matilda.' The burial ground is only a stone's throw from the chapel and so it's no time at all before you're all examining the gravestones. 'Sir George Oastley . . . Sir Walter Oastley . . . Captain Horace Oastley,' Miss Crumble reads out eagerly as you pass from one to another. 'Here we are – Matilda Oastley! Born 1713, died 1790.' There's an old marble urn at the foot of Matilda's gravestone, and Miss Crumble immediately thrusts in her hand, hoping to find the diamonds inside. While she doesn't pull out any diamonds, she does pull out a large blue key!

If you don't already have it there, put the BLUE KEY into your FOLDER. Now go to 270.

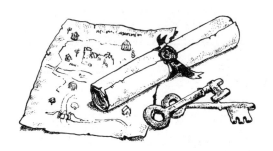

52

You just manage to shut the door behind you in time, locking it again from the inside. You forget that ghosts can walk through doors! But the squeaky footsteps now disappear, leaving you in peace. While you're in the room, you decide you might as well have a quick look round for the diamonds. The rows and rows of dusty books along the walls show that you're obviously in the library. 'Perhaps one of the books will have a secret hole cut into its pages!' the Professor remarks hopefully as you brush the thick cobwebs from some of their spines. But after ten tedious minutes of examining the books, you decide to abandon the task. Inspecting every single one will take all night! *Go to 285.*

'The spirits would like *you* to go first, Professor Bones,' Miss Crumble softly informs him after she has studied her dice. Taking a big nervous gulp, he starts to descend the crumbling steps. As the rest of you follow him down into the dark, eerie chamber, it becomes clear that the Professor was right about it once being a dungeon. For the light from his candle suddenly flickers on some rusty manacles hanging from the stone walls. It is these manacles that your little group nervously examines first. 'Look at all these drawings and dates gouged into the wall behind them!' the Professor remarks. 'They must have been done by the wretched occupants of the dungeon to pass the time. I wonder, though . . . perhaps one of them is a clue from Sir Edward.'

Do you have the WILL in your FOLDER? If you do, check whether any of the gouged drawings shown below are included there – then follow the appropriate instruction to find out Sir Edward's clue. If you don't have the WILL, go to 259 instead.

After cautiously pushing open the wide doors, you discover that Professor Bones was right. This *is* the banqueting room. There's a very long oak table in the centre, with a candelabra on it. Of course, both are covered with thick, trailing cobwebs. You notice that there's also a large silver dome on the table. Miss Crumble explains that it was used for covering a joint of meat. You both suddenly have the same thought. Perhaps it now covers the diamonds! But when you race each other to lift the dome, you find that there is just a mouldy bone underneath. 'No, you can't have it, Spooks,' Miss Crumble says with a wag of her chubby finger. 'It will give you a bad tummy, as you well know!' *Go to 205.*

Sir Edward's clue tells you to return to the stairway and investigate the thirteenth step down. So you all quickly start to descend the tower again, convinced that you're going to be discovering the diamonds any minute now. You're even more convinced when you examine part of the wall just above the thirteenth step. One of the stones there is very loose! With great excitement you ease the stone out and find that there is a small hole behind. You all hold your breath as Professor Bones inserts his skinny hand. He doesn't pull out the diamonds, unfortunately, but he does pull out another plan of the estate. Oh well, better than nothing!

If you don't already have it there, put the PLAN into your FOLDER. Now go to 289.

**When you have recovered from this haunting, record it on the
GHOST COUNTER. Now go to 34.**

57

With great excitement you lift the lid of the chest, but then you
discover that there's only a moth-eaten blanket inside. 'See what's
underneath it,' Miss Crumble impatiently urges you. 'With all
those lumps, it looks as if it's covering something.' Yes, but *what*,
you wonder as you begin to do as she asks. Perhaps the blanket is
covering a skeleton! But then, it could be the diamonds. So,
shutting your eyes, you quickly whip the blanket away. 'What is it,
Miss Crumble?' you ask, still not daring to look. It obviously takes
her a while to look herself . . . but eventually she replies. 'I'm afraid
it's just Sir Edward's hunting clothes,' she sighs. *Go to 155.*

58

Your little group now starts to make its way nervously up the long
curving driveway. You keep to the centre, not sure what might be
lurking in the trees on either side. Perhaps it's just the wind that's

making them sway and rustle, or perhaps it's something else! Through the fading light, you notice a small lake coming into view on your left. 'Maybe we should have a quick search there for the diamonds,' you propose somewhat hesitantly. 'We don't know that they're definitely in the house. They could be hidden anywhere on the estate.' But who is to lead the way towards the eerie lake? Miss Crumble again suggests using her spirit dice . . .

Throw the SPIRIT DICE – then turn to the appropriate number.

If ☠ thrown   go to 225

If 🦇 thrown   go to 302

If 👻 thrown   go to 142

59

Miss Crumble gives the verdict you were dreading. The spirit dice has decided that *you* should lead down the eerie steps! Insisting that the others keep right behind, you start to descend the narrow stairway. It feels icy cold and smells strongly of damp. You're about halfway down when you suddenly hear a rustling noise slowly coming towards the top of the steps. It sounds like a long, heavy dress trailing across the floor! Panic-stricken, you all hurry to the bottom of the stairway. But your path is then blocked by a door.

And it's locked! You're going to need the right key, and FAST, because the rustling is now coming *down* the steps towards you!

Do you have either of the KEYS in your FOLDER? If you do, place it exactly over the door's 'lock' below to see whether it works – then follow the instruction. (You may try both KEYS if you have them.) If you don't have either of the KEYS – or your KEY doesn't work – go to 215 instead.

'Phew, what a relief!' you exclaim as you all now push the heavy trap-door back again and climb out. 'I thought we were going to be stuck down there for ever!' In fact, your relief is so great that it takes everyone a while to notice Spooks. Something is dangling from between his teeth. 'The diamonds!' Miss Crumble suddenly cries with delight as she's the first to glance down at her little dog. 'Oh, clever, modest little Spooks! He must have found them somewhere in the dungeon!' You and Professor Bones join Miss Crumble in giving Spooks an ecstatic pat on the head. You can now all leave this terrible place!

Well done! But don't forget the rumour that there is more than one diamond necklace hidden in Ghostly Towers. If you would like to attempt to find the others as well, you must start your exploration again from the beginning. Try setting off with a different ITEM next time.

The Professor starts climbing again, the rest of you only a couple of the slippery steps behind. It's not long before he reaches another wooden shutter hinged to the stone wall. 'There must be an open window behind this one as well,' he deduces, scratching his shiny head. 'I suggest we try and locate this second window on the plan of the estate. It should show us how high up we are – and therefore how much further there is to go!

Do you have the PLAN in your FOLDER? If you do, use it to find which square the tower's second window is in – then follow the appropriate instruction. If you don't have the PLAN, you'll have to guess which instruction to follow.

If you think A1	go to 99
If you think B1	go to 168
If you think B2	go to 251

Your first haunting! When you've recovered from the shock, record it on the GHOST COUNTER. Now go to 231.

63

'It *is* just a bush!' you say with a sigh of relief as the next flash of lightning suddenly illuminates the sky. You're only given a very quick glimpse of it but you're quite certain now that it's not a ghost! A deafening clap of thunder rumbles round the mansion, making Spooks's hair stand right up on end. Oh, why didn't you check the weather forecast before setting out? But you did! It said that it would definitely be calm this evening. Perhaps it *is* everywhere else . . . perhaps Ghostly Towers has a storm just to itself! *Go to 34.*

64

Your stomach tight with tension, your hands clammy, you now lead the little group into the heart of the cellar. Your footsteps echo eerily on the stone floor and cobwebs seem to claw at your face. The place is icy cold and damp and a horrible smell of mould fills your nostrils. You can hear a slow drip of water from somewhere. 'Let's make our search here as quick as possible, shall we?' you whisper over your shoulder, barely able to find your voice. 'This has to be the scariest part we've been to in Ghostly Towers. And that's saying something!' *Go to 296.*

65

Your little group quickly leaves the boathouse and starts to walk round the shadowy lake. You have gone some hundred metres or so when Spooks suddenly starts to sniff round the reeds down at the water's edge. 'What have you found, Spooks?' Miss Crumble asks, waddling behind him to investigate. 'Goodness me, it's an old iron box. Maybe this is where the diamonds are hidden!' The box is firmly locked, though, and so needs a key to open it . . .

Do you have either of the KEYS in your FOLDER? If you do, place it exactly over the iron box's 'lock' below to see if it works – then follow the instruction. (You may try both keys if you have them.) If you don't have either of the KEYS – or your KEY doesn't work – go to 134 instead.

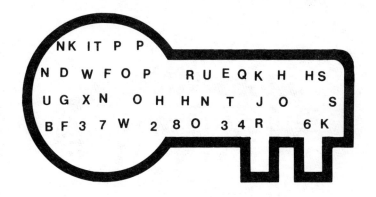

66
The clue in Sir Edward's will tells you that it will be to your advantage to step off the driveway and explore the grounds to the right. 'Do you think that means that's where the diamonds are hidden?' Miss Crumble asks, the large beads round her neck trembling with her excitement. But the Professor is more cautious. 'Perhaps it just means that we'll find more keys and things there,' he mutters thoughtfully. 'Still, if they're going to be of assistance in uncovering the diamonds, we really ought to have them. So let's take Sir Edward's advice, shall we?' It's with considerable trepidation that you all leave the driveway for this corner of the grounds. The trees are quite dark and thick there, almost like a wood . . . *Go to 77.*

Sir Edward's clue tells you to turn left twice and right once. 'I hope this is not a little joke of his to get us lost in the maze,' you remark as you all follow his instruction. You suspect this even more when the three turns take you to a dead end. But then Spooks starts sniffing under the tangled hedge here. You all hold your breath as he starts to dig, hoping he has found the diamonds. Unfortunately, he hasn't . . . but he does unearth a large red key. And at least you now know that Sir Edward wasn't just trying to get you lost!

If you don't already have it there, put the RED KEY into your FOLDER. Now go to 122.

When you have recovered from this haunting, record it on the GHOST COUNTER. Now go to 97.

Passing through the gate, you all cross the little footbridge. It makes a horrible creaking sound underfoot, but you're relieved to find that it *does* go all the way to the other side! 'It's a very brave dog you've got there, Miss Crumble,' the Professor comments to her pleasantly as they step off the bridge. 'Most dogs are terrified by the supernatural. I know a Rottweiler that shakes like a baby if you mention the word *ghost*.' Miss Crumble looks proud but Spooks seems to want to tell the Professor that *he* is shaking as well. It's just because he's so small it's harder to notice! *Go to 101.*

70

You're suddenly distracted by a piercing scream from Miss Crumble. 'What is it, Miss Crumble?' you ask, quickly turning in her direction. 'You haven't seen a ghost down the well, have you?' To your relief, she shakes her head. 'No, dear child,' she replies with a sob. 'I just had another look in this bucket to make sure the Professor hadn't missed something. You really might have warned me, Professor. There's a great big toad sitting at the bottom!' *Go to 264.*

71

You decide that you don't really like Miss Crumble's spirit dice because it apparently determines that YOU should be the one to try the gates. But you're reluctant to argue with it and so you tentatively start to turn the large iron ring. You feel your blood run cold as the gates slowly creak open. You've now pushed them just wide enough to pass through . . . but Professor Bones asks you to wait a moment while he examines the plaque bearing the family crest on the gatepost. He's wondering if the design includes one of those strange drawings in Sir Edward's will. In other words, a CLUE!

Do you have SIR EDWARD'S WILL in your FOLDER? If you

*do, check if any part of the family crest below is included there –
then follow the appropriate instruction to find out his clue. If you
don't, go to 84 instead.*

72

Even though now unlocked, the coach door still needs a really good
tug to open it. 'How luxurious!' Miss Crumble exclaims as you all
squeeze into the padded interior. 'This must have been the coach
that Sir Edward and Lady Rowena used for their really special
occasions. Like going to a royal ball.' You and the Professor are not
really listening to Miss Crumble, though, since you're busily feeling
under the faded red velvet seats for the diamonds. 'I think I've
found something!' you cry as your fingers touch something right in
the corner. When you slide it out, however, you find that it is just a
tiny, moth-eaten glove. It must have been Lady Rowena's! *Go to
92.*

73

When you realise that you unfortunately didn't bring the plan of the
estate with you, Miss Crumble looks quite cheerful about it! 'The

time we were going to spend studying the plan,' she says, 'I can now use to examine the gravestones instead!' So she has her way after all! She's only just started peering at the inscriptions on the stones, however, when the little bell at the very top of the chapel starts to ring. You're terrified! None of you dares look up in case it's a ghost causing this. But then you persuade yourselves that it's probably just the wind. So you slowly lift your heads . . . *Go to 138.*

When you have recovered from this haunting, record it on your GHOST COUNTER. Now go to 101.

'I wonder whether it would be better to leave this front door open or closed?' the Professor asks. 'The problem with leaving it open is that it will allow any ghosts to escape. But if we close it, they might feel trapped and therefore remain hidden. So I think it would probably be better to leave it open.' *A likely excuse!* You know full well that the real reason Professor Bones wants to keep the door open is so that you can all make a speedy departure if any ghosts appear! But, as it turns out, he has no choice in the matter as the door suddenly slams shut in the fierce wind. Since you can't find anything heavy enough to wedge it open again, you just have to leave it like that. **Go to 159.**

76

'It's chosen *you* this time, Professor Bones!' Miss Crumble informs him after she has studied the roll of her spirit dice. So the nervous Professor starts to climb the broad staircase, the rest of you a couple of stairs behind. When he finally reaches the top, he leads the way along the shadowy landing to a half open door right at the end. 'This must have been one of the guest rooms,' he whispers anxiously as he steps inside. 'It's much too small to be the master bedroom.' Walking round the musty-smelling bed, the Professor takes his flickering candle to the window. It's in a deep alcove which must be the little turret you saw from outside, at the corner of the building. The Professor suggests locating the turret on the plan of the estate so you know exactly where you are in the mansion.

Do you have the PLAN in your FOLDER? If so, use it to find which square the turret is in – then follow the appropriate instruction. If not, you'll have to guess which instruction to follow.

If you think C2	go to 171
If you think C1	go to 127
If you think D1	go to 294

The trees seem to grow thicker and thicker as you make your way amongst them. The dead leaves noisily crunch and crackle beneath your feet. 'This is probably where Sir Edward did his hunting,' the Professor says as his eyes nervously flit from side to side behind his spectacles. His theory seems to be confirmed by the sight of a small wooden hut a short distance ahead. It's presumably a hunting lodge. You all hurry up to it, agreeing that it would be an ideal place to hide the diamonds. But when you reach the door, you find that it is firmly locked. 'I wonder if one of those keys would unlock it?' the Professor asks pensively.

Do you have either of the KEYS in your FOLDER? If you do, place it exactly over the hut's 'lock' below to see if it works – then follow the instruction. (You may try both keys if you have them.) If you don't have either of the KEYS – or your KEY doesn't work – go to 221 instead.

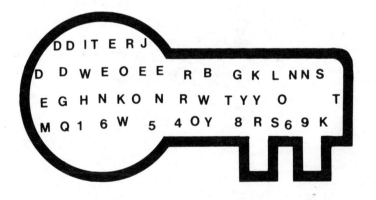

Sir Edward's clue tells you to forget about this door and to go to the one in the large tower at the back of the mansion. 'Do you suppose that means the diamonds are hidden there?' the Professor asks eagerly as you all hurry round the house. Reaching the strange tower at the back, you're convinced that the heavy oak door will be impossible to open. The huge hinges look as if they have rusted solid. But, although they make a loud creaking noise, they still just about work. The door very slowly moves . . . and Miss Crumble nervously leads the way into the cold dark tower. *Go to 247.*

79

Warily looking from side to side, your little group now starts to follow the long, curving driveway. Shadowy trees whisper and sway all about you. 'Are you sure there are no guard dogs patrolling here?' the Professor asks, trembling so much that his glasses keep slipping down his nose. 'I thought I could hear something padding over the fallen leaves to our left.' Miss Crumble reminds the Professor what Mr Creak told you, however. He's never been able to find a guard dog brave enough to patrol the grounds! *Go to 188.*

80

You eagerly pull the wardrobe door open and look inside. 'What beautiful gowns!' Miss Crumble exclaims. 'At least, they probably *were* beautiful before the mould and moths got at them. Lady Rowena must have had such style!' Forget Lady Rowena's style, though . . . what about the diamonds? Unfortunately, they're nowhere to be found in the wardrobe. So you start to search the rest of the room, looking under the bed and checking through all the drawers. You even pat the musty pillows to check if the diamonds have been sewn in there. 'They must be somewhere else in the mansion,' says Professor Bones dejectedly, a good ten minutes later. 'This is just like looking for a needle in a haystack, isn't it?' *Go to 199.*

When you have recovered from this haunting, record it on the GHOST COUNTER. Now go to 22.

82

You all hurriedly squeeze through the door and lean back hard against it as soon as you're on the other side. 'Press as hard as you can!' the Professor urges desperately. 'Even though her slow movement probably means it's the ghost of quite an old woman, she might have surprising strength. Age doesn't make much difference with ghosts!' Fortunately, though, the rustling sound grows quieter again as if the ghost has turned round and climbed back up the steps. 'Who do you think it was?' you ask, breathing slightly more easily. Professor Bones scratches his head but Miss Crumble is sure she has the answer. 'Mrs Grimes!' she proclaims dramatically. 'Sir Edward's formidable housekeeper!' *Go to 64.*

83

With everyone tense in expectation, Miss Crumble flicks up the box's lid. It is indeed a jack-in-the-box. For out jumps a large, mischievous puppet, springing towards the Professor's nose! But is there anything else inside the box? Yes, there is! Sparkling away at the bottom of the box is a necklace – the most beautiful necklace you've ever seen. It's the diamonds! You carefully take out the necklace with a delighted grin. A relieved one too. Your exploration of this terrifying mansion is finally over!

Well done! But don't forget the rumour that there is more than one diamond necklace hidden in Ghostly Towers. If you would like to attempt to find the others too, you must start your exploration again from the beginning. Try setting off with a different ITEM this time.

84

Since you haven't brought Sir Edward's will with you, however, there's no way of telling if there's a clue hidden in the crest. You're just about to lead the way again, through the gates, when you hear something further along the stone wall. 'Is this our first haunting?' you ask with a tremble. 'I think it might well be,' Miss Crumble whispers, her body suddenly being taken over by a strange spasm. 'I didn't hear anything but I can sense it. I can sense it . . . oh yes, I can sense it!' *Go to 37.*

You haven't walked far from the well when you reach a rather strange glass building. It looks a bit like a greenhouse, but more round in shape and it has a long wooden seat inside. 'My guess is that it's a little summer-house,' Professor Bones remarks. 'They were for keeping you warm when the sun was out but there was a bit of a chill in the air. People used to take their afternoon tea in them.' This summer-house doesn't seem like a bad place for hiding the diamonds in, so you walk round to the little glass door. When you test the handle, though, you discover that it's locked! 'I wonder if one of those two keys would unlock it?' the Professor asks, scratching his bald head . . .

Do you have either of the KEYS in your FOLDER? If you do, place it exactly over the 'lock' below to see if it works – then follow the instruction. (You may try both keys if you have them.) If you don't have either of the KEYS – or your KEY doesn't work – go to 312 instead.

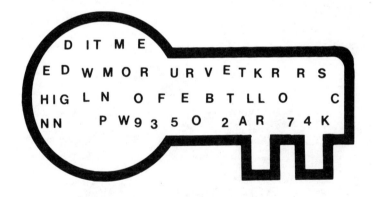

Your little group now reaches the weeping willow, its flimsy branches gently dancing in the wind. 'Such a pity it isn't a ghost!' the Professor sighs. 'I was really getting quite excited about it.' Then why was his skinny body shaking so much, you wonder. Shaking with excitement? 'Have you met a lot of ghosts in your work, Professor Bones?' you ask him doubtfully. 'I expect they run into

the hundreds, don't they?' The Professor lets out a shrill chuckle.
'Oh, my dear child, of course I have,' he reassures you. 'I meet them
virtually every day.' If that's true, you can't help thinking, then why
won't he look you straight in the eye! *Go to 231.*

Unfortunately, of course, you don't have the estate plan with you.
So it wasn't such a good idea of the Professor's after all. 'We'll just
have to try and guess which direction the driveway is in,' you decide.
You have walked only a short distance from the maze, however,
when you suddenly hear the sound of clipping from that direction.
It sounds as if someone is cutting the hedges! Could it be the ghost of
Sir Edward's gardener? Maybe his spirit has become so restless
about how untidy the maze has become that it has decided to make a
brief return! You all nervously look back over your shoulders . . .
Go to 12.

**When you have recovered from this haunting, record it on the
GHOST COUNTER. Now go to 46.**

When you have recovered from this haunting, record it on the
GHOST COUNTER. Now go to 17.

90

Unfortunately, of course, you chose not to bring the estate plan with
you. So there's no means of telling whether this seat is three-quarters
of the way along the driveway, or just a quarter. You certainly can't
see the end of the driveway yet. The path just disappears into the
rapidly-fading light. It's from somewhere beyond where the path
disappears that you suddenly hear the sound of horses' hooves!
Could it be one of those ancient carriages Miss Crumble mentioned?
You all freeze as the sound grows louder. You're expecting the
carriage to appear any second now . . . *Go to 206.*

91

But then you remember that you didn't bring the plan of the estate,
so your little trio leaves the well. But the Professor looks as if he
wants to stay. 'You know, I've still got this feeling that the diamonds
are there,' he says, frowning as he walks along. 'Just because they

weren't in the bucket . . . For all we know, they might be sitting at the bottom of the well. If only one of us could get down there and take a . . .' He suddenly stops in his tracks as his eyes rest on Spooks. It's quite plain to you what he's thinking. They could lower Spooks down in the bucket! But it's also quite plain to Spooks and he runs for cover behind the nearest tree. Miss Crumble is just about to tick the Professor off for his tactless ideas when you all suddenly hear a loud sighing noise behind you. It's coming from the well . . .
Go to 182.

92

You're still wandering through the grounds and you are all becoming rather concerned about how dark it is getting. Unless you find the mansion soon, you won't stand a chance! Only a few minutes later, however, through the darkening mists, you spot its spooky towers bathed in an eerie moonlight. It's the creepiest sight you've ever seen! 'Look, there's still a flag flying from one of its towers,' you remark with a gulp. 'How strange, after all these years. Can you see that emblem on it? I wonder if part of it is one of Sir Edward's clues?'

Do you have the WILL in your FOLDER? If you do, check whether any part of the flag's emblem is included there – then

follow the appropriate instruction to find out Sir Edward's clue. If you don't have the WILL, go to 49 instead.

93

Since you don't have the estate plan with you, however, you begin your search of the stables immediately. They're all very disappointing! You've just entered the last one when you think you hear the sound of horses' hooves on the cobbled exercise yard outside. It can't be! But then the sound comes again, a little louder this time. Is it the ghost of one of Sir Edward's stable lads taking a horse for a brief trot? You all crouch behind the lower half of the stable door and very slowly start to crane your necks so you can peep over the top. You hope and pray that there's a more rational explanation for this sound . . . **Go to 132.**

94

Since you chose not to bring Sir Edward's will with you, however, you'll never know whether one of his clues is hidden on the flags. Your little group leaves the chapel to explore the other parts of the estate, but you've walked only fifty metres or so from the eerie building when you hear something that makes your hair stand right up on end. Organ music! Is there a ghost sitting at that little dusty organ you saw in the chapel? You all force yourselves to go back to the chapel, tentatively peering in through one of the broken windows. Your eyes move slowly towards the corner with the organ . . . *Go to 163.*

95

When you have recovered from this haunting, record it on the GHOST COUNTER. Now go to 313.

96

After making a big sweep round the edge of the lake, the driveway at last brings you in sight of the mansion itself. 'No wonder people have nicknamed it *Ghostly* Towers!' you exclaim, as you peer at the spooky-looking turrets bathed in a dull moonlight. 'Whoever would want to live in a house like that?' But come to think of it, whoever would want to *explore* a house like that! Just as you did at the gates, you look to Professor Bones and Miss Crumble for some reassurance. But – just as they were then – they are trembling as much as you! *Go to 140.*

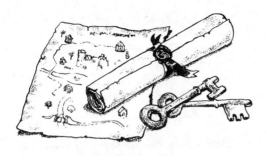

Professor Bones suggests that you leave the driveway for a while so you can explore the corner of the estate over to the right. 'It is essential that we search every centimetre for the diamonds,' he says. You agree with him, although you can't help wondering if the real reason for his suggestion is simply to put off reaching the mansion for as long as possible! As it turns out, though, this area is probably just as scary because you soon find yourselves in a dark, eerie wood. Fir trees whisper and sway all around you. 'Let's see if we can work out where we are from the plan of the estate,' the Professor suggests with a shiver.

Do you have the PLAN in your FOLDER? If you do, use it to find which square the fir trees are in – then follow the appropriate instruction. If you don't, you'll have to guess which instruction to follow.

If you think C4	got to 238
If you think D4	got to 5
If you think C3	got to 204

After taking her time to interpret the roll of the spirit dice, Miss Crumble's plump face relaxes with relief. This is bad news for you and the Professor. It obviously means that the dice has chosen one of *you two* to go first up the dark stairway. But who? 'I'm afraid it's *you*,

Professor Bones,' Miss Crumble announces softly. Your dome-headed, nervous friend has led you up about thirty of the stone steps when he suddenly stops. 'Look, there's a large wooden shutter here,' he says, holding his candle to it. 'There must be an open recess behind. But I wonder if the diamonds are there too, hidden in the stone recess?' When he tries to swing the wooden shutter open, however, he finds that it is firmly locked.

Do you have either of the KEYS in your FOLDER? If you do, place it exactly over the shutter's 'lock' below to see whether it works – then follow the instruction. (You may try both KEYS if you have them.) If you don't have either of the KEYS – or your KEY doesn't work – go to 297 instead.

Of course, you chose not to bring the estate plan. You're just reminding the Professor about this when you realise it hardly matters anyway – you can see a crack of sky above you. The top of the tower is only a few more steps. As you emerge into the howling wind, however, you find that it was all just a waste of time. There's absolutely nothing up there, diamonds or anything else! So you start the long climb down again but you've only descended half a dozen steps when you suddenly hear an agonised cry from the top. You all nervously look up, hoping it's just the wind . . . *Go to 50.*

100

Sir Edward's clue tells you that the diamonds are *not* hidden in any of the books. 'Well, it's not as helpful a clue as we'd hoped for,' Miss Crumble remarks disappointedly as she returns the dusty volume to the shelf. 'But I suppose it's better than nothing!' She then starts slowly to inhale the library's musty air, closing her eyes. 'You know, I can sense Sir Edward's presence quite strongly in here,' she says softly. 'This was obviously his favourite room. Do you think I should try and make contact with him and ask for a better clue?' You, the Professor and Spooks all vigorously shake your heads, though. The library is spooky enough without Miss Crumble going into one of her trances! ***Go to 236.***

101

Several hundred metres beyond the lake, your little group reaches an old stone well. 'Mm, how interesting!' the Professor remarks. 'This must have been where the mansion obtained its water. That means we must be quite close now, although I can't make it out yet through the dusk.' It suddenly occurs to you that you might not have to go as far as the mansion, though. Down this well would be a wonderful hiding place for the diamonds! 'Perhaps the necklace is in the bucket at the end of the chain,' you tell the others excitedly. 'We can find out by turning this handle to bring the bucket up!' But none of you is very keen on turning the well's handle. What if you bring up a little ghost instead! 'Since there are no volunteers,' Miss Crumble says, 'we'll let my spirit dice pick someone, shall we?'

Throw the SPIRIT DICE to decide who this poor person is to be.

If ☠ thrown		go to 31
If 🦇 thrown		got to 243
If 👻 thrown		go to 172

102

When you have recovered from this haunting, record it on the GHOST COUNTER. Now go to 166.

103

You remind the Professor that you didn't bring the estate plan with you, however. 'Oh no, of course not . . .' he mumbles. You have a sneaking feeling that he knew this all along but was just looking for an excuse to delay a few seconds more. How could it possibly help knowing which direction the mansion faces, anyway! Just at that moment the door suddenly slams shut behind you, blown by a violent gust of wind. You all jump with fright. But then there's an even bigger fright – an eerie tapping starts on the other side of the door. Is it just an overhanging branch causing this, or is it something much worse? Miss Crumble tensely opens the door a slight crack to find out . . . *Go to 44.*

104

To your immense relief, the ghost completely ignores you all, passing through the locked door. 'What a shame he didn't open it for us,' Miss Crumble remarks. 'A gentleman would have done!' But it would seem that the ghost *was* a gentleman after all. For, when you try the door again, you find that it is unlocked! This completely changes Miss Crumble's opinion of the ghost. 'I *thought* there was something gentlemanly about him,' she says as you all return to the stairway. 'He had a certain bearing. The next seance I have, I think I might well ask him to pay a visit. We could have a nice chat over some tea and cakes!' *Go to 331.*

105

Your nervous little group now creeps along the dark landing towards another door. This one is much wider, a double door, in fact. It's also much more ornate, with gold decoration. 'This must be the master bedroom,' Miss Crumble says as her fingers lovingly touch the faded gold. 'Sir Edward would have wanted only the very best for his darling Rowena!' She turns the beautiful gold knob but finds that the door is securely locked. 'I wonder if one of those two keys will fit?' she asks eagerly.

Do you have either of the KEYS in your FOLDER? If you do, place it exactly over the door's 'lock' below to see whether it works – then follow the instruction. (You may try both KEYS if you have them.) If you don't have either of the KEYS – or your KEY doesn't work – go to 194 instead.

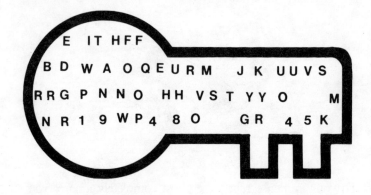

106

There's yet another fork of lightning at the window as you all leave the music room. You quickly close the door on the eerie pink flash. Even the darkness of the hall seems preferable to that! But you can't close out the thunder that follows. It seems to rumble at the mansion's very foundations, making the walls tremble. You all jump as a decorative sword suddenly comes loose, dropping down just to your left. You only hope that the same doesn't happen to a dusty stag's head, staring down from high above you. Those antlers look quite lethal! *Go to 178.*

107

Sir Edward's clue tells you that you are wasting your time searching the drawing-room for the diamonds: they are hidden somewhere else in the mansion! 'Come along, Spooks!' Miss Crumble calls from the door. 'You can't sit admiring that painting of Sir Edward all night. We've got other rooms to explore.' But Spooks wasn't admiring the painting, he was quietly growling at it! He didn't like Sir Edward and all his silly little clues. Why didn't he just hang the diamonds on the front gate for all to see? That would save having to come inside this spooky mansion! *Go to 178.*

108

When you have recovered from this haunting, record it on the GHOST COUNTER. Now go to 289.

109

Thankfully, the horrible apparition stops just before she reaches you. She then turns round, climbs slowly back to the top of the steps, and wanders off towards another part of the house. 'That must have been Mrs Grimes, Sir Edward's housekeeper,' says Miss Crumble breathlessly. 'Do you recall Mr Creak telling us about her? He said that she was very strict with the maids and they were all afraid of her. I expect her ghost was coming down to check there was enough wine in the cellar but suddenly remembered a more important duty upstairs.' While Miss Crumble is talking, you try the cellar door again. Mysteriously, it is no longer locked! *Go to 64.*

110

It *is* a raven, though, much to your relief. The large glossy bird comes flapping down the stairway, but is quite startled by your presence. You must be the first human beings it's ever encountered in the tower, and Spooks must be the first dog it's met there as well. For it flaps straight back to the top of the tower again, terrified as Spooks starts to bark at it. Little Spooks seems rather proud of himself at this. They are the noisiest barks he's ever done! Of course, it's probably just because of the echo in the stairway. But no one is going to tell Spooks this. Best to keep him thinking he really is fierce in case you meet any ghosts! *Go to 61.*

111

Just before leaving the chapel area, you think you had better quickly search the little graveyard nearby. You rather get the impression that the Oastley family had an odd sense of humour. These eerie tombs and crosses might have seemed to them an amusing hiding place! As you're warily stepping between the gravestones, Miss Crumble suddenly calls your attention. 'Come and have a look at this one, loveys,' she says. 'Algernon Frederick Oastley. Look, just above his name there are some strange symbols carved into the stone. I wonder if one of them is a clue from Sir Edward?'

Do you have the WILL in your FOLDER? If you do, check whether any of the symbols carved into the gravestone below are included there – then follow the instruction to find out Sir Edward's clue. If you don't have the WILL, go to 18 instead.

112

You're just about to check your folder to see if you brought the estate plan with you when you sense something watching you from the very top of the gateposts. You daren't look up. Could this be your first haunting, already? Whatever it is moves a little, creating a slight breeze which sends shivers down your spine. You can't stay rooted here for ever, though. You're going to have to lift your head and look . . . ***Go to 201.***

113

Without Sir Edward's will, however, there's no way of telling if one of the symbols on the fountain is actually a clue. You're all just about to leave the fountain when there's a gurgling sound from the jug the maid is holding. Presumably, the water used to spurt out of here . . . but not now, surely, after all these years? Unless the fountain is haunted, of course! You all slowly lift your eyes towards the maid's face. You have a horrible feeling that she is coming to life . . . **Go to 234.**

When you have recovered from this haunting, record it on the GHOST COUNTER. Now go to 199.

Miss Crumble's eyes slowly lift from the spirit dice, fixing gravely on the Professor. 'I'm afraid it has decided on you, Professor Bones!' she tells him. 'It is you who must go and investigate the dark figure!' The Professor seems quite nervous at the prospect but he does his best to hide it. 'It will be my pleasure, madam,' he says, as he leaves with a determined stride. 'Let's just hope it is a ghost. I've had so many disappointments over the years!' As it turns out, this is another disappointment for the Professor (although, you have to say, he doesn't sound that disappointed!). For he is soon shouting back to you all that Miss Crumble was right; the figure *is* just a statue. When you've joined the Professor at the statue, he suggests locating it on the plan of the estate.

Do you have the PLAN in your FOLDER? If you do, use it to find which square the statue is in – then follow the instruction. If you don't, you'll have to guess which instruction to follow.

If you think C4	go to 180
If you think D4	go to 97
If you think D3	go to 19

116

'It's just a young deer!' you say with a sigh of relief as you cautiously poke out your head. Professor Bones tugs at his little beard. 'How strange!' he comments. 'I wonder what it's doing in a place like this? I suppose it must be a descendant of one of Sir Edward's herd. Although it's quite remarkable after all these years. It just shows how undisturbed the grounds must have been!' The deer quickly disappears into the trees as you all leave the hut, squeezing out through the window. *Go to 20.*

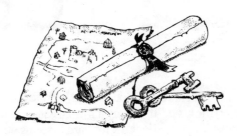

117

Miss Crumble's spirit dice chooses Professor Bones to go first down the narrow stairway. So he slowly starts to descend the crumbling steps, feeling his way along the damp stone wall. Finally reaching the bottom, he leads you all into the echoing darkness of the cellar.

'Let's make our search as quick as possible,' he suggests in a nervous whisper as the light from his candle flickers across rows of dusty wine bottles. Suddenly, the candlelight picks out a tall cupboard in the corner. 'This is probably where the more valuable drink was stored,' the Professor says as you walk over to it. 'The brandy and the vintage port. With any luck, it will be where the diamonds are stored as well!' But when you try to open the cupboard, you find that it is locked . . .

Do you have either of the KEYS in your FOLDER? If you do, place it exactly over the cupboard's 'lock' below to see whether it works – then follow the instruction. (You may try both KEYS if you have them.) If you don't have either of the KEYS – or your KEY doesn't work – go to 196 instead.

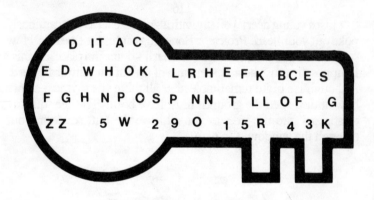

118

'No, of course I believe you, dear child,' Professor Bones says, patting you on the head. 'If you say it's just a willow, then it is just a willow. It's just that I'm so looking forward to seeing our first ghost, that I suppose I'm letting my imagination run away with me!' But as you walk a few steps nearer the eerie lake, you begin to change your mind about the willow. It is a willow all right, but you're sure you saw something move just behind it! You go forward a few more steps, taking these much slower, eyes fixed on the tree . . . *Go to 62.*

119

As you enter the dovecot to conduct a quick search, the doves nervously fly off through the holes at the top. You're probably the first human beings they've ever seen here! 'They're not the original doves, of course,' the Professor remarks as he climbs the rickety ladder. 'Sir Edward's, I mean. At least, I hope they're not the original birds. If they are, then they must be spirits!' He starts to wobble on the ladder at this thought and so you suggest he comes down again. 'I'm sure the diamonds *aren't* up there, Professor,' you tell him, giving him a hand. ***Go to 92.***

120

You let out a huge sigh of relief on finding out that the white shape *is* just a swan. It was taking off in your direction and is now flapping directly over your heads. The fright has made you completely forget your reservation about the gate, and you join the others in clambering over it. Without any misadventure, fortunately! 'Of course, I knew that swan wasn't going to be a ghost,' Miss Crumble remarks as you now cross to the other end of the little footbridge. 'I would have had one of my sensations if it had been. But I couldn't feel a thing.' That's funny, you think. How was it then that she looked as petrified as the rest of you? ***Go to 101.***

121

But of course . . . you didn't bring the plan of the estate with you. Fancy forgetting that already! It just shows how nervous you're becoming. You soon have even more reason to be nervous. For, suddenly looming out of the darkness ahead, you see the eerie turrets of the mansion. Ghostly Towers itself! Your reluctant feet very slowly take you nearer. Some of the mansion's windows are now just about visible as they catch the moonlight. But is that the reflection of the moon in the window at the top left . . . or the glow of a white-clad figure? You close your eyes as you continue to walk nearer to the house. You're now about to open them again. And, when you do, you're going to know for sure about that glow at the window . . . *Go to 38.*

122

Some ten minutes after leaving the maze, you catch sight of a building in the eerie dusk ahead. To begin with, you think it's the house but then you realise that it's much too small. 'It's the stables!' Miss Crumble suddenly remarks as you move a little closer. You all agree that you must give the stables a quick search, but none of you really wants to take the lead. There's a strange atmosphere about the place. You can hear some of the stable doors banging in the wind and even after all these years there still seems to be a faint horsy smell. 'I'll let the spirit dice decide on someone to lead, shall I?' Miss Crumble suggests in a tense whisper.

Throw the SPIRIT DICE – then turn to the appropriate number.

If ☠ thrown	go to 9
If 🦇 thrown	go to 160
If 👻 thrown	go to 249

Miss Crumble's spirit dice apparently wants *you* to take the lead, and so, feeling very tense, you start to descend the crumbling steps. You find yourself entering a dark, echoing chamber and you have this horrible feeling that the professor was right about it once being a dungeon. Your fears are confirmed when your flickering candle suddenly lights up some rusty manacles hanging from the rough stone walls. They were obviously for chaining up prisoners! As your huddled little group now nervously explores the dungeon, you spot a long wooden box in the dark shadows. Could it be a coffin, perhaps containing the remains of a prisoner? But Professor Bones insists it's just a chest. When he tries to open it to prove himself right, however, he finds that it is locked.

Do you have either of the KEYS in your FOLDER? If you do, place it exactly over the box's 'lock' below to see whether it works – then follow the instruction. (You may try both KEYS if you have them.) If you don't have either of the KEYS – or your KEY doesn't work – go to 274 instead.

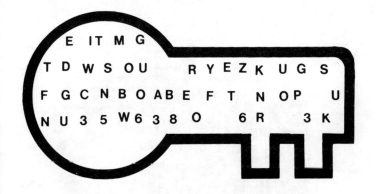

Since you don't have Sir Edward's will with you, Miss Crumble reluctantly returns to the business of opening the oak door. Or at least she tries to . . . but the door won't budge. 'I don't think it's because it's locked,' she pants as she puts her whole (and considerable) weight to the door. 'There seems to be something wedged behind it. A heavy table or cupboard.' Even with the three of you trying, the door still doesn't yield and so you decide to walk round the mansion to look for another entrance. It's as you're looking that you suddenly hear a whistling sound above you. It seems to be coming from the top of one of the chimneys. Perhaps it's just the wind forcing its way between the pots. You all nervously look up to check . . . ***Go to 202.***

125

You soon leave the music room and go back into the dark hall again. You've walked only a few steps from the door, however, when you all suddenly freeze with fright. The piano has started to play! 'But it was completely dead when I tried it a few minutes ago,' Miss Crumble stammers. 'And even if it wasn't, how can it play by itself?' Well, maybe it isn't playing by itself. Maybe there's a ghost sitting there! You nervously return to the music room door and open it very gradually. Your tense faces all peer through the narrow gap . . . ***Go to 322.***

126

When you have recovered from this haunting, record it on the GHOST COUNTER. Now go to 77.

You join Professor Bones at the little window to have a look out on the estate. You should get a good view from up here, but it's now so dark outside that it's impossible to see anything except your own reflection. It looks quite spooky as it flickers in the candlelight. You're just turning away from the window, however, when there's another flash of lightning outside. The whole estate momentarily lights up in an eerie shade of pink with black silhouettes looming everywhere. You rather wish you hadn't seen it after all! *Go to 105.*

Sir Edward's clue tells you to look up at the roof of the dungeon. With great curiosity, you do as it asks and study the rough, damp stone a metre or so above your heads. There's a large red key hanging there! Professor Bones immediately helps you on to his bony shoulders so you can reach it. 'I wonder what it's for?' the Professor asks as you wobble down to the floor again. 'It might merely be the key to the prisoners' manacles. Perhaps it was dangled here right in front of their eyes just to taunt them! But let's hope it has some other use. Something to do with the diamonds, for instance!'

If you don't already have it there, put the RED KEY into your FOLDER. Now go to 212.

Miss Crumble gravely informs Professor Bones that the spirit dice has chosen *him* to lead up the narrow stairway. With a large gulp, he graciously accepts the decision, and starts to climb the creaking steps. At the very top there's a tiny room, and as you tentatively enter, you realise that it was once the nursery. There's an old rocking-horse in the middle of the dusty floor and toy soldiers are scattered everywhere. The only window in the room is a tiny oval one, and you walk over to it to see how high up you are. But it's now so dark outside that it's impossible to tell. You're just turning away from the window when you notice some finger drawings in the thick dust. Could one of these be a clue from Sir Edward?

Do you have the WILL in your FOLDER? If you do, check whether any of the drawings shown below are included there – then follow the appropriate instruction to find out Sir Edward's clue. If you don't have the WILL in your FOLDER, go to 276 instead.

Miss Crumble peers down at her spirit dice, frowning at it for a moment. 'It's decided that *you* should be the one to go and investigate the shadowy figure, Professor Bones,' she tells him picking the dice up again. After the Professor has left you both, you ask Miss Crumble whether the spirit dice *really* decided on him – or did she just make it up! Her eyes almost pop out of her head and she looks as if she is about to give you an indignant earful. Fortunately, the Professor calls back to you at this moment, telling you that the figure *was* just part of a fountain after all. As you join him there, he suggests looking it up on the plan of the estate.

Do you have the PLAN in your FOLDER? If you do, use it to find which square the fountain is in – then follow the appropriate instruction. If not, you'll have to guess which instruction to follow.

If you think E1	go to 3
If you think E2	go to 219
If you think D2	go to 153

You seem to have no choice but to forget about the locked jack-in-the-box. Just as you're leaving the nursery, however, its lid suddenly flies open and a cheeky-looking puppet jumps out. 'Look, there's a note in its hand!' you exclaim when you've all recovered from the shock. 'I wonder if it's an important clue?' It's nothing of the sort, though. The note tells you to leave Ghostly Towers immediately or your sanity will be at stake! It's not the sort of warning any of you are inclined to take lightly, and so you all rush down to the front door and hurry back along the driveway towards the gates . . .

Your exploration of Ghostly Towers wasn't a success on this occasion. If you would like another attempt, you must start the game again from the beginning. Try setting out with a different ITEM next time to see if it gives you more luck!

When you have recovered from this haunting, record it on the
GHOST COUNTER. *Now go to 161.*

133

The clue in Sir Edward's will says that the raised crest should be pushed to the left. 'But how can it be?' the Professor asks, shaking his head. 'It's cemented to the gatepost.' You move up to the Professor's side so you can examine the crest more closely. You notice that it's not cemented at all but held there by a tiny screw at the top. And this screw also acts as a hinge, allowing the crest to be pushed up to the left. 'Look, there's a secret cavity behind!' you exclaim. 'And a red key inside!'

If you don't already have the ***RED KEY*** *there, put it into the slit of your* ***FOLDER.*** *Now go to 217.*

134

'Perhaps we should come back tomorrow with a crowbar,' the Professor suggests casually as you all stare down at the iron box, feeling very frustrated. 'The middle of the day would be a good time for me.' Miss Crumble gives him one of her reproachful looks. 'I'm sure it would, Professor,' she remarks. 'When it's nice and light, you mean, and there aren't so many ghosts about? Anyway, we would only be wasting our time. I've just had one of my "messages" from beyond. The diamonds are definitely *not* in this box.' You're just wondering how reliable Miss Crumble's messages are when you think you notice something move on the little footbridge at the far end of the lake. You'll be able to see it a lot more clearly in a second or two because the moon is just about to emerge from behind a cloud . . . *Go to 14.*

135

Miss Crumble looks quite faint as she peers down at the face of the dice. 'I'm afraid the spirits have decided that it's me who should try the gates!' she says quietly. She braces herself and slowly extends her shaking fingers towards the large iron ring. To Spooks's obvious relief, she finds the gates are locked. Perhaps they can all go home now! But Professor Bones suddenly remembers those two rusty keys. 'I wonder if one of them will unlock the gates?' he asks. The question is, did you bring a key with you?

Do you have one of the KEYS in your FOLDER? If you do,

place it exactly over the 'lock' below to see if it works – then follow the instruction. If you don't have either of the KEYS – or your KEY doesn't work – go to 36 instead.

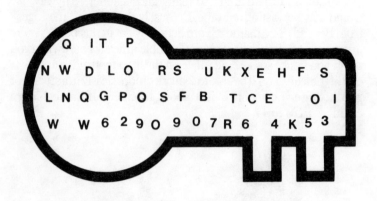

136

You're all just about to leave the seat when Spooks starts sniffing around underneath it. To begin with, you wonder if the ghosts of Sir Edward and Lady Rowena *are* sitting there with you. Perhaps Spooks has picked up their scent. But then you of course realise that if there was any hint of a ghostly presence, Spooks would be absolutely miles away! No, Spooks's interest is obviously a more down-to-earth one. You soon find out what. He has rooted out a large red key in the long grass under the seat, proudly dropping it into Miss Crumble's lap. He seems to be hoping that in return she will stop going on about Sir Edward and Lady Rowena!

If you don't already have it there, put the RED KEY into your FOLDER. Now go to 308.

137

Sir Edward's clue tells you to search the second stable from the left. You all immediately hurry towards this, hoping that you're going to be staring at the diamonds within the next few minutes. The bolt on the bottom half of the stable door is so rusted that it's impossible to pull back, but you all quickly help each other to clamber over the top. There's a horse's nosebag hanging in the far corner, and you're now absolutely convinced that the diamonds are in this stable, at the bottom of this musty old bag! There is *something* at the bottom of the nosebag but it's not the jewels, unfortunately. Just a lucky horseshoe. It's obviously Sir Edward's little joke! ***Go to 313.***

138

When you have recovered from this haunting, record it on the GHOST COUNTER. Now go to 270.

139

You forgot that you don't have the plan of the estate with you, however. So Professor Bones continues with his sneezing! Fortunately, there's something else to take his mind off it. 'What a marvellous church organ!' he exclaims as he strides through the cobwebs towards the other end of the chapel. 'It must be at least two centuries old. I wonder if it still works.' He's just about to sit at the little organ, however, when the stops start going in and out of their own accord. Then you hear music! You all hurry back to the chapel door and very slowly turn round to take another look at the mysterious organ. You're sure there's going to be a ghost sitting at it . . . *Go to 195.*

140

With hearts pounding, you approach the front door of the shadowy house. Crows squawk from the dark turrets above you and the windows rattle in the noisy wind. Ivy shivers against the crumbling walls. As the moon disappears again behind a racing cloud, you ask how you're going to see in the mansion. The gas supply would surely have been cut off long ago. That's assuming there ever was one, of course. 'I thought of that!' the Professor replies proudly. 'So I brought some candles and matches with me.' You would have much preferred a torch, but candles are better than nothing. Now all you have to do is choose who is going to enter the eerie house first. Miss Crumble suggests letting her spirit dice make that difficult decision . . .

Throw the SPIRIT DICE – then turn to the appropriate number.

If ☠ thrown   go to 224

If 🦇 thrown   go to 35

If 👻 thrown   go to 179

141

Miss Crumble's spirit dice apparently decides that *you* should now take the lead. You'd really like to know how she manages to work it out. The strange symbols seem completely meaningless to you! Anyway, you immediately take the candle from the Professor and warily beckon them along the cold dark hall. The flame makes eerie shadows flicker about in front of you. Suddenly you hear a deep voice from somewhere beyond the shadows. 'Good evening, sir,' it croaks quietly. 'Can I take your hat and cloak?' *Go to 267.*

142

This time the spirit dice decides that *you* should lead the way and you tentatively branch off the sweeping driveway. The mist-shrouded lake comes nearer and nearer. 'What's that standing at the edge?' the Professor asks anxiously at your shoulder. 'I have a terrible feeling it's a ghost . . . an exhilarating feeling, I mean.' Squinting through the dusk at the Professor's 'ghost', however, you realise it's just a tree. A weeping willow, in fact, its trailing branches looking rather like dangling arms. 'Are you sure it's just a tree?' Professor Bones asks, wiping his glasses. You give him your complete assurance, telling him to look for it on the plan of the estate if he doesn't believe you.

Do you have the PLAN of the estate in your FOLDER? If you do, find which square the lakeside willow is in – then follow the appropriate instruction. If you don't, you'll have to guess which instruction to follow.

If you think C2	go to 118
If you think C3	go to 86
If you think B3	go to 231

You all desperately barge through the door and quickly lock it behind you. 'Are you sure that it will stop him?' you ask the Professor anxiously. 'I thought ghosts could pass through locked doors.' The Professor suddenly turns red with embarrassment and then white with fear. He'd forgotten all about that! But, fortunately, the clonking sound on the other side of the door grows quieter again as if the ghost has changed his mind and is returning to the bottom of the stairway. It's only now that your little group realises that it's in the open air once more, the rain lashing down on you all. A few steps more and you reach the very top of the tower! *Go to 278.*

Pushing the double doors open, you find that the once elegant bedroom is now in an advanced state of decay. The four-poster bed is covered in cobwebs and smells badly of mould. When you touch the faded curtains, they disintegrate in your fingers! 'Just crawl underneath the bed and see if there's anything hidden there, will you, Spooks?' Miss Crumble asks her little dog. When he stubbornly refuses, she starts to look underneath it herself, lifting the musty bedspread. 'There are no diamonds down here,' she tells you as she splutters in the dust, 'but I have found *something*. It's another copy of Sir Edward's will!'

If you don't already have it there, put the WILL into your FOLDER. Now go to 199.

You now intend to return to the driveway but billows of thick eerie mist suddenly envelop your little group, causing you to walk in completely the wrong direction. The mist quickly clears again . . . but when it does you find yourselves by a very overgrown maze. 'These hedges really need a good trim,' Miss Crumble says fussily as she scratches herself on one of the long branches. 'They look as if they haven't been tended for years!' You and the Professor are more concerned with working out precisely where you are in the grounds, however. The Professor suddenly has an idea. 'Let's see if the maze is shown on the plan of the estate,' he says, his eyes lighting up behind his spectacles.

Do you have the PLAN in your FOLDER? If you do, use it to find which square the maze is in – then follow the appropriate instruction. If not, you'll have to guess which instruction to follow.

If you think E2   go to 183
If you think E3   go to 87
If you think D3   go to 122

146

It seems that the wailing sound *was* just the wind because you can't see anything peeping over the top of the maze. A ghost could have quickly got down again, of course, but the Professor tells you that you can't count it as a genuine haunting unless you actually *observe* something. 'We ghostologists have very strict rules about this,' he continues pompously. 'Some people say that you can classify a rattle of chains as a haunting, or even a mysterious perfume, but they don't really know what they're talking about.' Well, you're certainly not going to argue with the Professor. If *he's* happy about not calling that wail a haunting, then so are you! ***Go to 122.***

Sir Edward's clue tells you to go to the fifth bottle from the left, three rows up. You quickly locate this wine bottle and take it from the rack. The cork hasn't been pushed all the way in. You can just get a grip on it, and you excitedly pull it right out. You then carefully turn the bottle upside down into Miss Crumble's cupped hands. For her sake, you hope there *isn't* wine in there. Out pours a string of sparkling diamonds. Even in the pale light of the candle, they look absolutely stunning. Your search of this terrifying mansion is over at last!

Well done! But don't forget the rumours that there is more than one diamond necklace hidden in Ghostly Towers. If you would like to attempt to find the others as well you must start your exploration again from the beginning. Try setting off with a different ITEM next time.

Sir Edward's clue tells you to *open* the window. As you tug away at the rusty handle, you're convinced that it's going to come off, but finally the window begins to loosen. 'Surely the diamonds aren't hidden out *here?*' you remark after one last tug gives you enough room to put your hand out. You feel along the stone ledge, afraid of what you might touch. There could be rats, or anything! 'Wait a minute, I think I've found something!' you exclaim as your fingers just reach a thin metal object. You carefully draw it back towards you. It's an old blue key!

If you don't already have it there, put the BLUE KEY into your FOLDER. Now go to 34.

Before you return to the driveway, you decide to explore the grounds over to the right. One thing that particularly interests you is a very overgrown maze! Agreeing that it would be an excellent hiding place for the diamonds, you all venture inside. 'I hope we'll be able to find our way out again,' Miss Crumble remarks hesitantly as you turn left and right, trying to reach the centre. 'One hears of people getting lost in these for days!' Well, at least you find the centre fairly soon: it is marked by a little obelisk. Noticing some strange carvings up the side of this stone monument, Professor Bones wonders if one of them might be a clue from Sir Edward.

Do you have the WILL in your FOLDER? If you do, check whether any of the symbols shown below are included there – then follow the instruction to find out Sir Edward's clue. If you don't, go to 220 instead.

150

Still honouring the decision of her spirit dice, Miss Crumble leads the climb over the gates. She's much more agile than you would have expected for one so ample. Apart from a few problems with the spikes at the top, she makes it all look quite easy and soon lands on the other side. Professor Bones is rather less nimble, his long spindly limbs more of a hindrance than a help, but he too eventually gets over safely. When you've reached the other side yourself, only Spooks is left. He tries to squeeze between two of the railings of the gates but he's just a bit too big. 'Come on, Spooks,' Miss Crumble chides him. 'I know you're not breathing in enough! If you don't squeeze through this very second, we'll just have to leave you there on your own until we come out again. I believe there's a headless figure that sometimes patrols these gates.' Before you can even so much as click your fingers, Spooks has joined you within the grounds! **Go to 79.**

151

'Bingo!' the Professor exclaims delightedly as the key opens the padlock. 'Look, there's a very old rowing-boat inside. Let's hope the diamonds are hidden in there and then we can immediately leave the estate . . . not that I don't find it absolutely fascinating, of course!' You're beginning to wonder if the Professor has actually *witnessed* a ghost before, or has he just done lots of research about them. For he seems no keener on lingering at Ghostly Towers than you do! But you're going to have to linger at least a bit longer, unfortunately, because your search of the rotting boat proves disappointing. All you find inside are a few stones! **Go to 65.**

152

When you have recovered from this haunting, record it on the GHOST COUNTER. (Don't forget: when you have recorded

four hauntings, you must immediately stop the adventure and start the game all over again.) Now go to 140.

153

'Come out of there, Spooks!' Miss Crumble orders her little dog as he suddenly jumps into the middle of the pool. 'If it's a wash you want, you're wasting your time. The fountain obviously hasn't worked for years and years!' But Spooks ignores his mistress, trotting up to the stone figure in the centre. It's a maid pouring a jug. Presumably, it was from this jug that the water once flowed, but it's not for that reason that Spooks is interested in it. He pops his head into the jug and pulls out a folded sheet of paper. 'Why, it's another copy of Sir Edward's will!' Miss Crumble exclaims as Spooks delivers it to her. 'Well spotted, Spooks. You're not such a disobedient dog after all!'

If you don't already have it there, put the WILL into your FOLDER. Now go to 3.

154

Because it's so rusty, the little iron door needs quite a lot of tugging to free it, but at last you all manage to pull it open. There is indeed a secret cavity behind! Miss Crumble immediately thrusts her chubby hand into the hole, so excited that she doesn't even care about scratching her many rings. 'Don't worry, my dearie,' she tells you. 'My rings are only imitation diamonds. Unless I'm much mistaken, there are going to be genuine ones lying inside here!' But, unfortunately, she *is* much mistaken because the secret cavity contains only a few cobwebs! ***Go to 17.***

You all now continue along the landing towards one of the rooms. It's a very large room with a huge four-poster bed in the middle. 'This must have been Sir Edward's and Lady Rowena's bedroom,' Miss Crumble remarks, as you push away all the trailing cobwebs. 'I expect it looked quite magnificent in those days.' With your candle creating eerie shadows on the ceiling, you tentatively make your way towards a large wardrobe against one wall. Perhaps the jewels are hidden in here! You tear away the cobwebs from one of the doors and start to turn the brass handle. You can't understand why it won't open but then you notice that it has a lock . . .

Do you have either of the KEYS in your FOLDER? If you do, place it exactly over the wardrobe's 'lock' below to see whether it works – then follow the instruction. (You may try both KEYS if you have them.) If you don't have a KEY – or your KEY doesn't work – go to 254 instead.

S S	I T	U	U
G W	D K O N R	E P K S	U W S
K N W G T O R A	D A	T V V	G O M
B F W 6	S O 5	Q R 4 8 N K 3 0

As you warily push open the hut's rotting door, you find that it is indeed a hunting lodge. For there are a couple of ancient guns propped up in the corner and some rusty traps hanging on the wall. But no sign of the diamonds! Your search of the cobweb-strewn hut isn't completely without success, though. For, just as you're about to give up, Spooks discovers a large blue key on the floor. 'Well done, Spooks,' you tell him, patting his little white head. 'This might be the key to the main door of the house!'

If you don't already have it there, put the BLUE KEY into your FOLDER. Now go to 20.

157

You open the lid of the bucket and quickly reach inside. But in your excitement you let go of the bucket just before your fingers touch the bottom. It swings back into the centre of the well and then slowly starts to descend, the chain unwinding again. 'Quick, grab the handle!' Miss Crumble orders. This you do, preventing the bucket's further descent. You start to wind it up again, promising to be much more careful this time. 'You hold the bucket, Miss Crumble, and I'll feel inside.' There are no near disasters this time . . . but no diamonds either! The bucket isn't completely empty, though. There's a large red key sitting at the bottom!

If you don't already have it there, put the RED KEY into your FOLDER. Now go to 207.

When you have recovered from this haunting, record it on the
GHOST COUNTER. Now go to 236.

159

You can't put it off any longer, you're now going to have to start your exploration of the deserted house! You're just debating who should take the lead when there's a sudden flash of light at one of the windows, accompanied by a deafening rumble. That's all you need – the start of a thunderstorm! As if the place wasn't spooky enough! The next flash of lightning is even brighter and you hear the crash of branches outside as it splits a tree in half. 'We'd better begin our search of the house immediately, while it is still in one piece,' Miss Crumble advises. 'We'll let my spirit dice decide who is to take the lead.'

Throw the SPIRIT DICE – then turn to the appropriate number.

If 💀 thrown	go to 13
If 🦇 thrown	go to 318
If 👻 thrown	go to 141

'Oh goody, it's me again!' Miss Crumble claps her hands with delight as she studies the roll of her spirit dice. You don't really believe her joy at the dice's decision, but at least she doesn't try and get out of it! As you follow her towards the eerie stables, the banging of the loose doors grows louder and louder. You only hope that it *is* the wind causing this! 'Before we start our search of each of the stables, let's try and find them on the plan of the estate,' Miss Crumble suggests on reaching the little exercise yard. 'It will tell us exactly where we are.'

Do you have the PLAN in your FOLDER? If you do, use it to find which square the stables are in – then follow the appropriate instruction. If not, you'll have to guess which instruction to follow.

If you think D2	go to 268
If you think E2	go to 93
If you think E1	go to 226

Not long after leaving the stables, your little group arrives at a derelict dovecot. As you peer up at the little holes at the top, you wonder if there are still any doves there, but they've obviously long since departed. It then occurs to you that up there would be a wonderful place to hide the diamonds! So you all walk round the

dovecot to find the entrance. 'Here it is!' the Professor exclaims on
reaching a little oak door. When you try to open the door, however,
you discover that it is locked. 'The lock looks about the same size as
those keys,' Miss Crumble remarks. 'I wouldn't mind betting one of
those would open it!'

*Do you have either of the KEYS in your FOLDER? If you do,
place it exactly over the door's 'lock' below to see whether it
works – then follow the instruction. If you don't have either of the
KEYS – or your KEY doesn't work – go to 208 instead.*

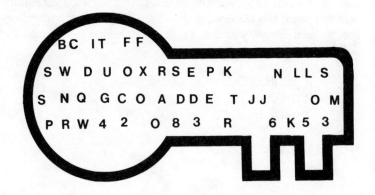

162

'Perhaps we can slide the window down and get into the coach that
way?' Miss Crumble suggests as you all stare, disappointed, at the
locked door. But the window won't budge, and you really don't
want to smash it in case a sharp edge gives one of you a bad cut as you
crawl through. So you just have to be content with pressing your
faces up to the window, judging what you can from there. 'There's
certainly nothing on the middle of the seats,' the Professor says, with
his nose squashed sideways. 'But it's difficult to see right into the
corners.' As you all try your best, a velvet curtain is suddenly drawn
across the window! Did you jog it loose, or is there a spirit inside
wanting its privacy? You all leap back from the coach as the curtain
slowly starts to open again . . . *Go to 252.*

'Well, there's certainly nothing sitting there now,' you remark with relief as your eyes rest on the organ. 'Perhaps the ghost has finished playing and has gone to haunt somewhere else!' But then the organ music softly starts up again. 'You know, I don't think it's the work of a ghost after all,' the Professor says, having recovered from his initial shock. He gives his beard a little tug. 'I think it's just the wind forcing itself down the organ-pipes. I'd like to believe it was a ghost, of course. But my reputation is based on the fact that I'll always consider the rational explanations first!' ***Go to 270.***

When you have recovered from this haunting, record it on the GHOST COUNTER. Now go to 104.

As Miss Crumble slowly lifts the lid of the box, you all hold your breath. Even Spooks! But your hopes are in vain because the box is completely empty. 'So I grazed my knee for nothing!' Miss Crumble says, tutting in annoyance. She holds out both her arms, one towards you and the other towards the Professor. '*Now* you two can help me up!' she says. You've just raised her to her feet again when the moon suddenly emerges from behind a mass of cloud . . . and you notice a huge black silhouette several hundreds metres to your right. It's the mansion! *Go to 140.*

166

To everyone's huge relief, the ghost suddenly turns away, disappearing through a wall. Spooks is especially relieved. The ghost seemed a very fussy one, the type that would give a dog a sharp kick! 'That was Sir Edward's butler all right,' the Professor says, wiping the beads of sweat from his brow. 'Well, he was certainly of that period. You could tell by his fuzzy whiskers and those large buckles on his shoes. I believe Mr Creak said his name was Baines, didn't he? He was obviously a very loyal soul. Did you see how ancient he was?' Professor Bones was right. The butler looked even older than he did! *Go to 285.*

167

'I was hoping it would decide on me!' Miss Crumble says cheerfully as she looks at how her spirit dice landed. You're not sure whether you believe her about this, but at least she didn't try and cheat! You and the Professor stick closely behind Miss Crumble as she opens the little wooden door and steps into the chapel's eerie interior. Cobwebs trail everywhere and a dusty mist swirls between the pews. You're searching the front of the chapel when you discover a tiny door built into the wall. It's less than a metre high. You try to open it, thinking this might be where the diamonds are hidden, but it is firmly locked . . .

Do you have either of the KEYS in your FOLDER? If you do, place it exactly over the door's 'lock' below to see whether it works – then follow the instruction. (You may try both KEYS if you have them.) If you don't have either of the KEYS – or your KEY doesn't work – go to 245 instead.

168

There's only one more twist of the stairway before you finally reach the top. As your little group emerges into the night air once more, the fierce wind howling all about you, Miss Crumble warns you against going too near the edge of the tower. 'That parapet looks quite unsafe,' she remarks. 'I wouldn't mind betting an Oastley or two slipped over at some time, and plunged to their dooms! Their ghosts probably still haunt the . . .' But you and the Professor shut your ears to Miss Crumble's unnerving chatter and have a quick look round. Since there's absolutely nothing here at the top of the tower, though – diamonds or anything else – you soon start the eerie climb down again. ***Go to 289.***

You've just given the drawers another good tug to see if they will come free without a key when you notice Spook's nose start to twitch. 'What is it, Spooks?' Miss Crumble asks with concern. 'Is this damp room giving you a chill?' But then you all realise that that's not the reason for his nose-twitching at all. There's a strong smell of perfume in the room! 'It must be Lady Rowena's!' Miss Crumble says as you all rush for the door and slam it shut behind you. 'Perhaps her ghost doesn't like us meddling with her dressing-table!' But when your nerves have calmed down a bit, you realise there's probably a much simpler explanation for the scent of perfume. You probably knocked an old bottle of it over when you were tugging at the drawers! So you confidently open the door again . . . *Go to 114.*

When you have recovered from this haunting, record it on the GHOST COUNTER. Now go to 199.

You remind the Professor that you don't have the estate plan with you, however. You and Miss Crumble are now just about to join the

Professor at the little window when it suddenly flies open. You all quickly crouch down behind a dressing-table. 'Oh, we're just being silly,' Miss Crumble says, after you've been cowering there for a minute or so. 'It was the storm that blew open the window. Listen to how fierce it is!' You and Professor Bones are sure she is right about this and you poke your heads above the dressing-table to get a look at the window . . . *Go to 228.*

172

The dice apparently decides that *you* should be the one to turn the handle. You can't really complain about this – after all, it was your idea to investigate the well! So you use both hands to grip the large wooden handle and it slowly creaks into action. Link by link, the chain starts to rise from the well's dark depths. 'I think this is the bucket coming now,' you eventually announce as something heavy clanks against the side of the well, causing an eerie echo. 'Yes, here it is!' As you reach for the old wooden bucket, though, you notice that it has a lid, and that the lid is held down by a lock. 'Do we have either of those keys with us?' you ask excitedly. 'Maybe one will fit the lock. I'm convinced the diamonds are hidden inside this bucket!'

If you do have either of the KEYS in your FOLDER, place it exactly over the 'lock' below to see if it works – then follow the instruction. (You may try both keys if you have them.) If you don't have either of the KEYS – or your KEY doesn't work – go to 286 instead.

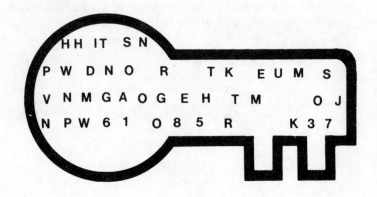

173

It is just an owl up there! Or, at least, there *was* an owl but your arrival scares it away. As its huge white wings flap towards a nearby tree, you all start to breathe again. 'So much for your ghost of Sir Edward, Miss Crumble!' Professor Bones says with a chuckle. 'It wasn't him that was calling out at all – to Rowena or anybody else. He'd spotted her in the gardens indeed! It was just that old owl hooting into the night!' The Professor was wrong to mock Miss Crumble so much, though. *He* had believed her as much as you had! *Go to 289.*

Since you're unable to open the secret door, you decide it would be better to go back and look for the Professor. You can't think what's happened to him. He must have been so impatient to find a ghost in the house that he wandered off without you. But remembering how nervous he was, though, that doesn't seem very likely! Perhaps there's a more serious reason for his disappearance. Perhaps one of the ghosts suddenly spirited him away! Just as you're running back into the hall, however, you hear a loud banging from behind that secret door. And a few seconds later, it starts to open . . . ***Go to 193.***

Your first haunting! When you have recovered from the shock, record it on your GHOST COUNTER. Now go to 2.

Having left the stables, you soon find yourselves approaching a strange little brick building. It has six sides and a pointed roof. There are also a number of holes in the upper part of the building. 'What can it be?' you ask. The Professor and Miss Crumble really have no idea, shaking their heads. But then you hear a cooing sound from inside the building. For a horrid moment you think it might be a ghost . . . until a dove flies out! 'Of course, it's a dovecot!' the Professor exclaims. 'Lots of large houses had them in the old days. Let's locate it on the plan of the estate so we know exactly where we are.'

Do you have the PLAN in your FOLDER? If you do, use it to find which square the six-sided building is in – then follow the appropriate instruction. If not, you'll have to guess which instruction to follow.

If you think D2	go to 288
If you think D1	go to 119
If you think E1	go to 316

177

Professor Bones is just turning away from the window when he notices an old red key lying amongst the cobwebs on the sill. 'Ah-ha!' he exclaims, picking it up. 'Now, I wonder if this is the key to the cupboard or drawer where the diamonds are hidden?' At that moment, though, there is another sudden clap of thunder outside and the Professor drops the key in shock. You've never seen such a bag of nerves! You're tempted to ask why he isn't more used to thunder and lightning, given how many haunted houses he must have investigated. But you tactfully refrain, helping him to find the key again. 'Here it is, Professor!' you announce, after feeling round the dusty floor.

If you don't already have it there, put the RED KEY into your FOLDER. Now go to 34.

178

Continuing your exploration of the ground floor of the mansion, your little group eventually finds itself at a bolted door tucked away in a corner. Drawing back the bolt and opening the door, you find some narrow stone steps behind. They lead not up, but down! 'They must go down to the cellar,' Professor Bones says with a gulp. 'That would be an excellent hiding place for the diamonds. So I think we'd better go down there!' The question is, who is to lead down the dark, scary steps? Since there are no volunteers, Miss Crumble says her spirit dice will decide . . .

Throw the SPIRIT DICE – then turn to the appropriate number.

If ☠ thrown	go to 117
If 🦇 thrown	go to 28
If 👻 thrown	go to 59

179

'The spirit dice has decided on *you*, my dear!' Miss Crumble informs you with a kind hand on your shoulder. As you nervously step right up to the arched oak door, you ask her if the dice ever chooses Spooks. 'No, only humans,' Miss Crumble replies. Glancing down to your left, you see a smug grin on Spooks's face! 'I hope this front door is going to open after all our trouble,' you remark as you reach towards its iron handle. 'These hinges look so rusty that I'm worried it might be permanently jammed.' Your fears appear to be justified – the door won't budge! But then you notice the lock just below the handle. Perhaps it simply needs the right key.

Do you have either of the KEYS in your FOLDER? If you do, place it exactly over the door's 'lock' below to see whether it works – then follow the instruction. (You may try both KEYS if you have them.) If you don't have either of the KEYS – or your KEY doesn't work – go to 21 instead.

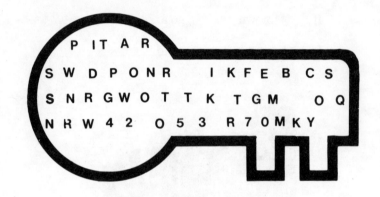

180

'So you have lots of disappointments in your sort of work, Professor?' you ask as your little group leaves the statue. 'Oh yes!' he replies. 'Lots and lots! You wouldn't believe how often I've been called out to a haunted house or church, merely to find that it wasn't haunted at all. Many a time it's just been the water-pipes clonking or a bird trapped in the attic. I remember one occasion when . . .' This is all very fascinating but you're rather more interested in the times when there genuinely *was* a ghost. 'There have been those times, haven't there, Professor?' you check, feeling a tiny bit doubtful. Professor Bones gives one of his shrill chuckles. 'Yes, of course!' he replies. 'Hundreds, my dear child, hundreds!' The odd thing is, however, that he chooses not to tell you about any of them, suddenly changing the subject. Perhaps it's just that he doesn't want to frighten you. *Go to 97.*

Opening the tiny door, you find that it is to give access to the workings of the fountain. 'How fascinating!' says Professor Bones as he bends down to take a look. 'I've always been interested in this sort of thing. You see, this little pump here forces the water . . .' But Miss Crumble stops him with an impatient tut. 'This is no time for a science lecture, Professor,' she tells him. 'All we want to know is whether the diamonds are hidden in there.' The Professor thrusts his hand in as far as it will go and wiggles it around a bit. 'No, Miss Crumble,' he replies with a sad shake of the head. 'I'm afraid they're not!' *Go to 149.*

When you have recovered from this haunting, record it on the GHOST COUNTER. Now go to 264.

'Do you think we should explore the maze?' Miss Crumble asks. 'Maybe the diamonds are hidden somewhere inside.' You and the Professor are not very keen on the idea, however. You might never find your way out again! 'Oh, don't worry about that,' Miss Crumble reassures you. 'My little Spooks here will get us out again. He just has to pick up our scent.' You wonder if there's another way of putting her off. 'Some of those brambles are awfully prickly, Miss Crumble,' you tell her after thinking for a moment. 'They'll ruin your nice cardigan.' Your ploy works. For Miss Crumble suddenly decides the diamonds aren't likely to be in the maze after all! *Go to 122.*

184

Well, you've managed to silence Miss Crumble for a moment, but it's now the Professor who starts to give you goose pimples! 'Yes, I know of a haunted lake too!' he tells you both. 'Well, not a lake exactly, a moat. It surrounds Blackstone Castle. Legend has it that on the first day of the month a hound can be heard whining across the water.' The Professor suddenly stops, pricking up his ears. 'Good heavens! I think I can hear a hound whining here!' Well, he's right in a way. The hound is poor Spooks, who's had quite enough of these frightening tales! *Go to 101.*

185

As the Professor is browsing lovingly through some of the dusty books, it suddenly occurs to you that one of them might be hiding the diamonds! 'Maybe there's a fake book here!' you suggest excitedly. 'One that is made to look like a book but is really a small box.' So you all eagerly scan the titles, wondering whether one will provide a clue: *The Secret Hideaway*, for instance, or *The Surprise*

Hollow. 'How about this title?' Miss Crumble exclaims after a while. '*More than Meets the Eye*. Perhaps that means the *book* is more than meets the eye!' As you quickly open it, however, you find that there are just normal pages inside. But what about that illustrated inscription at the front? Could it contain one of Sir Edward's clues?

Do you have the WILL in your FOLDER? If you do, check whether any part of the book's inscription shown below is included there – then follow the appropriate instruction to find out Sir Edward's clue. If not, go to 250 instead.

186

The will's clue tells you to seek elsewhere for the diamonds. 'A good job we found that out,' Miss Crumble remarks. 'I was just thinking about lowering one of us down in the bucket to search round the bottom of the well.' *You* think it was a good job too – you're the lightest of the three! Your little trio is just about to walk on from the well when Spooks starts sniffing at the long grass growing round it. 'What is it, Spooks?' Miss Crumble asks. 'Has mummy's clever little dear found something?' Spooks doesn't seem to like being called that . . . but yes, he *has* found something! 'It's another plan of the estate,' Miss Crumble informs you as she takes it from him. 'It's not too faded either. It must have been dropped here quite recently, probably by someone else who came looking for the diamonds. I expect they're now lying right at the bottom of the well. Stone dead!'

If you don't already have it there, put the PLAN into your FOLDER. Now go to 85.

187

'What *is* a summer-house, anyway?' you ask as you all now enter the little glass hut. The Professor tells you that it was where the rich used to sun themselves. 'You see, the glass maximises the effect of the sun's rays,' he explains learnedly. 'It's a process called . . .' But Miss Crumble suddenly interrupts him. 'Oh, do be quiet, Professor Bones!' she tells him. 'We've come here to look for ghosts and diamonds, not to have a boring little lecture.' The Professor seems rather hurt by this put down, blinking away behind his spectacles, but Spooks fondly rubs his head up against his shin. *He* would prefer a boring lecture to searching for ghosts any day! *Go to 22.*

188

You've been following the driveway for a good ten minutes but there's still no sign of the house. True, you haven't exactly been walking very fast, but you would have expected to have spotted it by now. The grounds are obviously massive! Peering into the dusk ahead, you suddenly see a shadowy figure standing to one side of the driveway. Is it your first ghost already? 'No, I don't think so,' Professor Bones says, trying to reassure you after giving his spectacles a good wipe. 'I believe it's just a statue standing in the middle of a fountain!' In order to make absolutely sure, Miss Crumble suggests someone runs up to the shadowy figure. 'I'll use my spirit dice to decide who,' she says.

Throw the SPIRIT DICE – then turn to the appropriate number.

If ☠ thrown	go to 130
If 🦇 thrown	go to 319
If 👻 thrown	go to 290

189

When you have recovered from this haunting, record it on the GHOST COUNTER. Now go to 92.

The spirit dice again decides that *you* should be the one to lead the way. 'I'm truly sorry about that, dear,' Miss Crumble tells you sympathetically, 'but fate is fate, I'm afraid. I can't do anything to change it!' You nervously walk up to the little wooden door of the chapel, which makes a horrible creaking sound as you open it. The interior is strewn with cobwebs and has a horrible quietness about it. Professor Bones starts to sneeze because of all the dust. You try to think of something to take his mind off it. 'Let's locate this chapel on the plan of the estate, shall we?' you suggest.

Do you have the PLAN in your FOLDER? If you do, use it to find which square the chapel is in – then follow the appropriate instruction. If you don't, you'll have to guess which instruction to follow.

If you think E3	go to 210
If you think D3	go to 139
If you think D4	go to 195

The wind comes swirling through the deep oblong hole as the Professor eagerly pulls open the shutter. That's not the only thing that comes in, however. A large bat flits right past the Professor's nose! But Spooks scares it back out again, pretending to be much fiercer than he really is. 'All right, that's enough now, Spooks,' you say as his deafening barks echo up and down the stairway. 'The bat went out a good minute ago!' You now turn your attention to the Professor, asking if he has found anything in the stone recess behind the shutter. 'Not the diamonds,' he replies a little disappointedly, 'but I did find *this* hidden under a loose part of the stonework. It's another copy of Sir Edward's will!'

If you don't already have it there, put the WILL into your FOLDER. Now go to 61.

The clonking noise is quite definite now. It sounds like someone slowly climbing the steps after you, dragging a ball and chain behind them. You quickly try to open the door as the eerie clonking grows louder and louder, nearer and nearer. To your horror, you find the door is locked!

Do you have either of the KEYS in your FOLDER? If you do, place it exactly over the door's 'lock' below to see whether it works – then follow the instruction. (You may try both KEYS if you have them.) If you don't have either of the KEYS – or your KEY doesn't work – go to 310 instead.

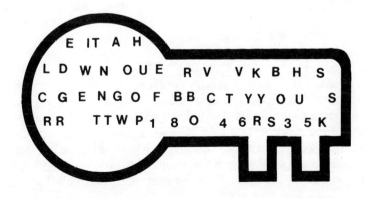

'Professor Bones!' you and Miss Crumble exclaim with relief as your thin friend steps out from behind the secret door. 'What happened to you?' The Professor scratches his domed head in confusion. 'I'm not really sure,' he answers vaguely. 'I couldn't resist going back to the library to have another look at those wonderful books. When I leaned on part of the shelving, I was suddenly spun round into a secret passage. Since I couldn't work out how to make the shelves rotate back again, I walked along the passage until I reached this door. It needed a good push, but it finally came open.' So you didn't need a key for the secret door after all. It was unlocked all the time! *Go to 178.*

You all decide to take a run at the double doors to see if you can try and force them open. But they remain firmly in position. All you gain from your efforts are very sore shoulders! As you're rubbing them, you suddenly hear a dripping sound from further along the landing. To begin with, you assume it's just a leaking tap but then the Professor points out that they probably wouldn't have had taps in those days. 'They would have got their water from the well in the grounds,' he says, as you all nervously walk towards the sound to investigate. The dripping is now only a few metres away; just the other side of a half-open door. Is it *blood*, you wonder as you peep into the room . . . ***Go to 305.***

When you have recovered from this haunting, record it on the GHOST COUNTER. Now go to 248.

'Sir Edward must have kept it locked to stop the servants pilfering the drink,' Miss Crumble says as you all try to *force* the cupboard open. But the sturdy door just won't budge! You're just having one last tug at it when Spooks starts to growl. 'What is it, Spooks?' you ask anxiously, hoping that it's just a rat he's spotted. You don't really like rats, but they are slightly better than ghosts! But then you realise that he has heard someone coming down the stone stairway. For, you can now hear the hollow footsteps as well. They belong to someone very slow and doddery. Could it be the ghost of Sir Edward's butler, you wonder with bated breath, as the intruder is about to appear . . . ***Go to 257.***

You remind the Professor that you don't have the estate plan with you, however. You're sure he knows this full well, but just wanted an excuse to delay exploring the dungeon for a few moments! That excuse now gone, you all begin your nervous search. 'Fancy being chained up in this horrible damp place,' Miss Crumble remarks as you edge past the dangling manacles. 'I bet prisoners were just left here until they rotted!' Wishing Miss Crumble would keep her thoughts to herself, you're at least relieved that there are no skeletons in the manacles. Or are there? For, as you continue your exploration, all huddled together, you're sure you hear the manacles suddenly rattle behind you! You all nervously look back over your shoulders . . . *Go to 222.*

'The dice has chosen *you* again, my dear!' Miss Crumble informs you gently. So you ask Professor Bones for the candle and carry its flickering light ahead of you all, up the stairs. When you finally reach the top, you nervously peer along the shadowy landing, wondering whether to go left or right. You decide on left, nearly tripping over a large chest in the middle of the floor. You're just about to walk round it when you realise that your search for the diamonds might not have to go a centimetre further. They might be *inside* this chest! So you ask the Professor to hold the candle for a moment while you crouch down to try and heave open the lid. 'Oh no, it's locked!' you say with a sigh.

Do you have either of the KEYS in your FOLDER? If you do, place it exactly over the chest's 'lock' below to see whether it works – then follow the instruction. (You may try both KEYS if you have them.) If you don't have either of the KEYS – or your KEY doesn't work – go to 272 instead.

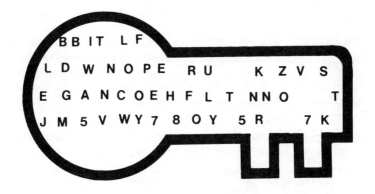

199

You're just about to return to the ground floor of the mansion when you notice that Spooks is missing! 'Oh, my poor little darling!' Miss Crumble cries. 'I hope one of the ghosts hasn't got him! Perhaps he's even now a ghost himself!' But then you hear Spooks's excited bark from the shadows further along the landing; he's obviously found something. 'Look, it's another stairway!' Miss Crumble remarks after she has given Spooks a suffocating hug. 'It seems to lead right to the top of the mansion, to the attic rooms. We'd better go and see what's up there.' But no one is very keen to lead up the stairway. It is much narrower than the main staircase, the steps steep and bare. After about the eighth step they disappear into complete darkness! 'We'll let my spirit dice decide who is to lead,' Miss Crumble suggests.

Throw the SPIRIT DICE – then turn to the appropriate number.

If ☠ thrown		go to 129
If 🦇 thrown		go to 306
If 👻 thrown		go to 218

200

You have to remind Professor Bones that you don't have the plan of the estate with you, however. Honestly, his memory is quite appalling! He's just turning away from the tiny window when he lets out a sudden shriek. 'Look! There's a dark figure standing below!' he exclaims. 'He must have noticed our candle flickering away. It's Sir Edward's ghost, I'm sure!' Rushing over to the window yourself, however, you're not so sure that it is a person down there. It could just be an ornamental bush. You decide to wait for the next flash of lightning. Then you'll know for certain . . . ***Go to 63.***

'Oh, it's just an owl!' the Professor exclaims with obvious relief as it flaps its large wings at the top of the gatepost. Watching it take off, he lets out a sigh. 'What a shame!' he remarks. 'I was really hoping it was our first encounter with the spirits.' You rather have the impression that Miss Crumble and Spooks believe the Professor no more than you do! *Go to 58.*

202

When you have recovered from this haunting, record it on the GHOST COUNTER. Now go to 332.

203

The gates give a blood-curdling creak as Miss Crumble slowly pushes them open. Nervously walking through, she insists that you and Professor Bones keep close behind. She doesn't have to bother telling Spooks; he's certainly not going to be left there on his own! 'I say, what's this?' the Professor suddenly asks after noticing something at his feet. 'Why, it's a plan of the grounds! That suggests someone else has recently come here in search of the diamonds. It looks like these gates were as far as they got. Something obviously scared them into dropping the plan and running off!'

If you don't already have it there, put the PLAN of the estate into your FOLDER. Now go to 79.

204

Of course, it was only a few minutes ago that you told the Professor that you hadn't brought the plan of the estate with you. It just shows how nervous he is if he's forgotten already! Your little group hasn't ventured much further through the wood when Spooks suddenly starts rooting amongst the fallen pine-cones. A wide grin spreads across his face as he digs up a bone. 'Naughty boy, Spooks!' Miss Crumble chides him as you continue on your way. 'You don't know where that's been.' Or, more importantly, *who it belonged to*! For you suddenly hear a rustling sound back where Spooks had picked up the bone. Was the bone part of a skeleton, a skeleton that's now starting to complain? You all nervously turn round to find out . . .
Go to 43.

205

Your nervous little group next explores what must have been the drawing-room. There's a huge fireplace at one end and a group of dusty leather armchairs. Drawn across the windows are long velvet curtains, mottled with furry mould. 'Come and have a look at this painting on the wall,' you call to the others, pointing to a portrait of a man in hunting clothes. 'It must be Sir Edward.' As you're all examining the cracked painting, Miss Crumble wonders whether there might be one of Sir Edward's clues hidden in the picture. 'You may well be right, Miss Crumble!' the Professor says eagerly. 'Do we have his will with us?'

If you have the WILL in your FOLDER, check whether any detail in the painting is included there – then follow the appropriate instruction to find out Sir Edward's clue. If you don't have the WILL, go to 295 instead.

206

But, much to everyone's relief, a carriage *doesn't* appear. Perhaps that sound wasn't horses' hooves after all. 'Much more likely just to have been branches rubbing together in the wind,' the Professor says casually now his nerves have settled a little. 'Yes, there's the sound again. Quite definitely branches, I would say!' As you all rise from the garden seat to continue your walk up the driveway, you wish that the Professor had worked that out before. And that Miss Crumble would stop all this romantic talk about carriages and the like! *Go to 308.*

Your trio hasn't ventured much further from the well when you spot a greenhouse through the misty dusk ahead. 'How wonderful!' Miss Crumble remarks. 'I've always been a bit of a gardener myself, haven't I, Spooks?' Not as much as I would like, her little terrier seems to be thinking. He obviously enjoyed sitting in the garden, occasionally chasing the odd bird. Much more than he enjoyed hunting ghosts anyway! As you approach the little outhouse, you realise it's not a greenhouse after all. Although it's made of glass, it's much rounder than a greenhouse and with wooden seats inside. 'My guess is that it's a summer-house,' Professor Bones says. 'But we can always make sure by finding it on the plan of the estate.'

Do you have the PLAN in your FOLDER? If you do, use it to find which square the little glass hut is in – then follow the appropriate instruction. If you don't, you'll have to guess which instruction to follow.

If you think A2	go to 314
If you think A1	go to 187
If you think B1	go to 22

You're just turning away from the lock, feeling very disappointed, when you hear a clicking noise on the other side of the door. It's the sound of a key turning. *You* might not have the right one with you but it appears that someone else does! You all immediately take to your heels and run from the dovecot, only stopping when you are a safe distance away. Your four petrified faces peep out from behind a tree to see what emerges from the door. After a whole minute has passed, however, you wonder if the sound was just caused by the wind hissing through the lock. But then the dovecot door suddenly flies open . . . ***Go to 189.***

When you have recovered from this haunting, record it on the GHOST COUNTER. Now go to 155.

You start to search the chapel, looking under all the dusty pews. Spooks soon has so many cobwebs wrapped round his nose that his face is hardly visible! In spite of all your efforts, however, there's not a diamond to be found. As you sit down on one of the dusty pews to take a rest, you suddenly notice the old hymn books lying there. This sets you thinking. Maybe one of them has a secret hole cut into the pages and the diamonds are hidden inside! 'Brilliant!' The Professor congratulates you and you all quickly start to examine the crumbling books. 'They were quite fond of using books as hiding places in the olden days.' And, indeed, you *do* find a secret hole in one of the hymn books. But it's not the diamonds lying there, just a small flask of whisky. Sir Edward's, no doubt! ***Go to 111.***

The doors are too heavy to try and open without a key, so you decide not to search that room. You're just turning away when you hear a slight clanking behind you. It sounds like pieces of metal moving. 'Did you say that suits of armour have been known to come to life?' you ask the Professor anxiously, not daring to look. 'Can they suddenly start walking?' But Professor Bones is too shocked to reply. It looks as if the only way you're going to get an answer is to turn round and peer back down the hall . . . *Go to 299.*

After a good twenty minutes in this dark, eerie dungeon, you all decide that you've searched it for long enough. The diamonds would seem not to be here after all. So you return to the stone steps and start to climb back up to the trap-door. Just before you reach it, however, it suddenly slams shut! When you quickly try and push it back again, you discover something to make matters even worse. You hadn't noticed before, but there's a lock in the door – and a key has now been turned in it! If you want to get out of this horrible place, you're going to need the right key to unlock it!

Do you have either of the KEYS in your FOLDER? If you do, place it exactly over the trap-door's 'lock' below to see whether it works – then follow the instruction. (You may try both KEYS if you have them.) If you don't have a KEY – or your KEY doesn't work – go to 329 instead.

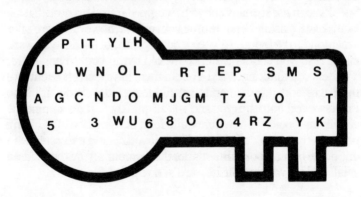

P IT YLH
U D WN OL   R F E P   S M S
A G C N D O M J G M T Z V O   T
5   3 W U 6 8 O 0 4 R Z   Y K

'But we didn't bring the estate plan with us, Professor Bones,' you remind him tactfully. 'So we didn't, dear child,' he says vacantly. 'So we didn't!' He now joins you and Miss Crumble in a quick search of the music room. You lift the rotting lid of the piano to check whether the diamonds have been hidden inside. But all you find in there is a startled mouse! The next thing you see is Miss Crumble standing on the piano stool, her skirt lifted to her knees. 'Quick, drop that lid down again!' she sobs, anxiously chewing her fingertips. 'I think we've searched this room quite enough!' You wonder what all her fuss is about. It's only a mouse she's seen . . . not a ghost! *Go to 125.*

With great excitement you jerk open the cupboard door and you all peer inside. Well, Professor Bones was certainly right about it being the place for storing the more valuable drink. It is full of bottles with rare, ancient labels. Some of them are now three hundred years old. But, of course, your real interest is the diamonds – could *they* be hidden somewhere amongst the bottles? You lift out the bottles one by one and look underneath. There aren't any diamonds, sadly, but your search is not completely unsuccessful. For, tucked underneath a large bottle of brandy, is another copy of the plan of the estate.

If you don't already have it there, put the PLAN into your FOLDER. Now go to 296.

When you have recovered from this haunting, record it on the GHOST COUNTER. Now go to 109.

216

While you and an irritated Miss Crumble give the padlock a good shake, the Professor wanders round to the side of the boathouse. 'Look, there's quite a wide crack here,' he exclaims. 'Wide enough for us to peer through!' As you all press your faces to the crack, Miss Crumble thinks she can just make something out inside. Now you and the Professor can see it too. 'It's a swan, I think,' you remark, squinting into the darkness. 'It's something white, anyway. We'll know for sure any second now because it's moving towards us . . .' *Go to 6.*

217

You nervously lead the little group up the long twisting driveway. Dark trees sway in the wind on either side, making a horrible rustling noise. 'I can't see the house anywhere yet,' you remark in a tense whisper as you peer into the dusk ahead. 'This driveway obviously runs quite a distance.' You then suddenly spot a dark figure standing on the right, about a hundred metres further up. 'Is it a ghost, Professor?' you ask with a gulp. But he seems even more petrified than you are and is unable to reply. 'I think it's just a statue,' Miss Crumble says eventually. 'One of us had better run up to it and make sure, though. I'll use my spirit dice to decide who it's to be!'

Throw the SPIRIT DICE – then turn to the appropriate number.

If 💀 thrown   go to 115

If 🦇 thrown   go to 223

If 👻 thrown   go to 307

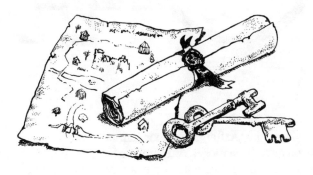

218

'It's *you* once again, my dear!' Miss Crumble tells you after she has rolled her spirit dice along the bottom step. You can't help feeling that it *always* seems to be you, but you graciously accept the dice's decision. Holding your breath in case you should accidentally blow out the candle, you start to mount the eerie steps. 'Be very careful how you tread,' you whisper back to the others. 'Some of these steps are badly rotten.' You all safely reach the top of the steps, however, and find yourselves on a small dark landing. There are two doors there, one to the left and one to the right. You turn towards the right one first, but when you try the handle you find that it is locked!

Do you have either of the KEYS in your FOLDER? If you do,

place it exactly over the door's 'lock' below to see whether it works – then follow the instruction. (You may try both KEYS if you have them.) If you don't have either of the KEYS – or your KEY doesn't work – go to 260 instead.

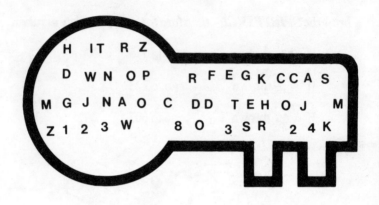

219

'But we chose not to bring the estate plan with us, Professor Bones,' you inform him tactfully. The poor man is obviously so brilliant that he has a terrible memory! You continue to walk along the driveway but you haven't got very far when you hear the sound of flowing water behind you. It seems to be coming from the direction of the fountain. Has it suddenly started to work again? If it has, then it must be haunted! You slowly turn your heads to find out . . . ***Go to 40.***

220

You now try to find your way out of the maze again. Miss Crumble insists that you all follow Spooks, saying that he'll be able to retrace your steps by picking up the scent. The trouble is he goes a bit too fast for you all. 'Wait, Spooks!' you cry as he dashes round one corner after another. 'We can't keep up!' It's not long before you've lost him completely! 'Don't worry, Miss Crumble,' you say to comfort her as she starts to sniff into her handkerchief. 'I'm sure he'll turn up again.' It's then that you hear a heavy panting sound a short distance behind you. You look round in horror. Something's just about to turn the corner of the hedge . . . **Go to 4.**

221

'I wonder if there's another way of getting into the hut?' Miss Crumble asks, strolling round to the back. 'Yes, there is! Look, there's a wooden flap here with an empty window-frame behind it. I think it's just big enough for us all to squeeze through.' Miss Crumble's large body nearly gets stuck, but by taking a deep breath even she manages to crawl through. The effort is a waste, though, because the hut is completely empty. You're just about to leave it again when you hear something move outside. 'W-w-what's that?' the Professor asks as you nervously lift the wooden flap at the window to take a look . . . **Go to 116.**

222

When you have recovered from this haunting, record it on the GHOST COUNTER. Now go to 320.

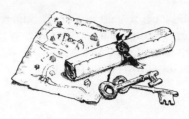

223

Miss Crumble goes quiet for a few moments as she looks down at her spirit dice. It's obvious that it has decided that *she* should be the one to investigate the dark figure. 'Well, I'm sure it *is* just a statue, anyway,' she says determinedly as she sets off up the path. 'Come on, Spooks!' But Spooks is remaining right where he is. As far as he is concerned, the spirit dice only selected his mistress to do the investigating; not him as well! But then he has a twinge of conscience and reluctantly starts to trot after her . . . ***Go to 237.***

224

'Whom has your spirit dice decided on, Miss Crumble?' the Professor asks nervously after she has tossed it on to the ground. He realises from her grave look that it must be him! With a brave shrug of the shoulders, he lights one of his candles, shielding its hesitant flame from the wind. He then turns the handle and pushes open the ancient oak door. The creaking sound echoes all the way through the dusty hall. 'Before we start our exploration of the mansion,' the Professor says, once you are all standing inside, 'I'd like to find out where this main entrance is on the plan of the estate. I'd be interested to know whether it faces north, south, east or west.'

Do you have the PLAN in your FOLDER? If you do, use it to find which square the main entrance of the mansion is in – then follow the appropriate instruction. If not, you'll have to guess which instruction to follow.

If you think C2	go to 75
If you think D2	go to 159
If you think D1	go to 103

'After you again, Professor!' Miss Crumble invites him when she has interpreted the roll of her dice. 'The spirits seem to like you for some reason!' You all follow him off the main driveway and start to trample through the crunchy fallen leaves towards the lake. The shimmer of water comes nearer and nearer, shrouded in an eerie mist. 'This must be where Sir Edward and the Lady Rowena did their early courting,' Miss Crumble says with a romantic sigh, as you reach a small wooden footbridge at one end of the lake. 'Look at all these initials and doodles carved into the handrail. They appear to be expressions of Sir Edward's love. I wonder, though, perhaps one of them is a clue from him!'

Do you have the WILL in your FOLDER? If you do, check if any of the carved doodles below are included there – then follow the appropriate instruction to find out Sir Edward's clue. If you don't, go to 277 instead.

'I expect Sir Edward was a superb rider,' Miss Crumble says dreamily as you now search the individual stables. 'And Lady Rowena too. I can just see her in her elegant riding outfit, coming to check the horses. Her favourite would probably have been called *Beauty* or *Silver Mist*.' Miss Crumble's imagination becomes so vivid that *you* can almost see Lady Rowena here too. And it's giving you the creeps! 'Let's just concentrate on looking for the diamonds for the moment, shall we, Miss Crumble?' you suggest tactfully. **Go to 161.**

227

The chapel door slowly creaks open as the Professor gives it a cautious push. The interior is even spookier than the exterior, cobwebs dangling from every beam and draping over the wooden seats. There's a small organ in the corner, which looks as if it hasn't been touched for centuries. You all stick very close together as you begin your search of the chapel. You peer under the seats and check down the back of the organ. You even check the dusty stack of hymn books to make sure nothing has been hidden in the spines. But the diamonds are absolutely nowhere to be found! **Go to 15.**

228

When you have recovered from this haunting, record it on the ***GHOST COUNTER****. Now go to 105.*

229

Crawling into the cavity behind the tiny door, you realise that it must have been some sort of hiding place. It's much too small for anything else. 'It was probably built in case an Oastley suddenly needed to hide from an enemy,' the Professor remarks knowingly. 'I expect the good priest would then hang a tapestry or something over the door to conceal it.' Of course, you're hoping that it is the diamonds that are now hidden in that secret nook. But you're to be disappointed. The only thing in there is a large spider! *Go to 46.*

230

There's a slow creaking noise as you push the heavy door open. 'We're in luck!' you exclaim. 'The door *isn't* jammed. Although these hinges could certainly do with a good oiling.' But as you all nervously squeeze inside the mansion, you wonder whether 'in luck' is the right expression after all. You certainly don't feel that lucky! It must be even worse for poor Spooks. At least you three humans have the prospect of the diamonds to compensate for your fear. But what use are diamonds to a little dog? He'd probably be much happier with an old bone! *Go to 39.*

You hurry along the lake, heading for the stream that flows into one end, where there's a little footbridge. The furthest end of the bridge is enveloped in such a thick greyish mist that it looks as if the bridge ends halfway across. But this is surely just an illusion. It *must* lead to the lake's other side. So you keep on walking. When you finally reach the bridge, you find there's a problem. There's a little wooden gate there, and it's firmly locked! 'Perhaps one of those keys will unlock it?' you suggest, searching your folder to see if you have either of them with you.

If you do have either of the KEYS in your FOLDER, place it exactly over the gate's 'lock' below to see if it works – then follow the instruction. (You may try both keys if you have them.) If you don't have either of the KEYS – or your KEY doesn't work – go to 263 instead.

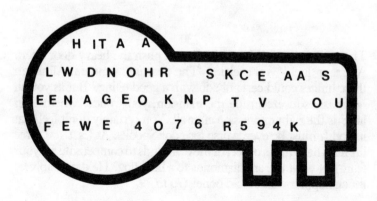

After cautiously pushing open the door, you walk into a tiny room with a low, sloping ceiling. The only window is a little oval one which is covered in cobwebs. There's an old rocking-horse in the centre of the room, also covered in cobwebs, and hundreds of toy soldiers scattered across the floor. 'It's a nursery!' Miss Crumble exclaims with delight as she waddles over to the rocking-horse and gives it a little push. 'Sir Edward must have played here when he was a little boy. Oh dear, what an untidy child he seems to have been!' *Go to 34.*

You give the little door a good shove and all enter the dovecot. It's very dark inside, and so you decide to make your search as quick as possible. 'I hope this is safe,' Miss Crumble remarks as she starts to climb a rickety ladder towards the top part of the building. Since she reaches it without mishap, you and the Professor start to climb the ladder as well. If it will take her weight, then it should certainly take yours! You all immediately check the holes through which the doves used to fly in and out while Spooks nervously keeps watch at the bottom. 'No diamonds, I'm afraid,' Miss Crumble announces shortly. 'But I have found *this*. It's another copy of the plan of the estate!'

If you don't already have it there, put the PLAN into your FOLDER. Now go to 92.

When you have recovered from this haunting, record it on the
GHOST COUNTER. Now go to 145.

235

The clue in Sir Edward's will tells you to search the bank
underneath the bridge. Miss Crumble immediately leaps down
there and gets on her hands and knees. 'Come and help, will you,
Spooks?' she asks. 'You're much better at this sort of thing than I
am.' But Spooks doesn't trust the underneath of the bridge and
stops right where he is! 'Don't be so silly, Spooks,' she tells him off.
'We won't find any ghosts down here.' But Miss Crumble doesn't
find anything else there either. It seems that Sir Edward was just
having a little joke! *Go to 2.*

236

Your little group eventually leaves the library, warily stepping out
into the hall again. You soon come to another door and you enter this
room; it's the grand dining-room. There's a very long oak table in
the middle, with fourteen straight-backed chairs around it. A

candelabra and empty port decanters sit on the table, both draped with heavy cobwebs. It's even gloomier than the library! Miss Crumble and you are just about to start to explore, when you suddenly realise that Professor Bones is missing! You were sure he was just behind when you left the library. ***Go to 41.***

'They've nearly reached the dark figure now,' the Professor says as you both squint after Miss Crumble and Spooks. 'I only hope she was right about it being a statue!' It appears that she was, though, because she is soon calling you both to join her. 'Nothing to be afraid of!' she tells you jauntily. 'It's just a stone effigy, of one of Sir Edward's ancestors, by the look of him. What a handsome figure of a man he was!' You must admit, you don't really find the ancestor that handsome – indeed, he looks a little mad – but, for the moment, you're more interested in the stone base of the statue. There's a rectangular iron plate there, with a keyhole in it. Could it serve as the door to a secret safe? Does one of those two keys fit the hole?

If you have either of the KEYS in your FOLDER, place it exactly over the 'lock' below to see if it works – then follow the instruction. (You may try both KEYS if you have them.) If you don't have either of the KEYS – or your KEY doesn't work – go to 265 instead.

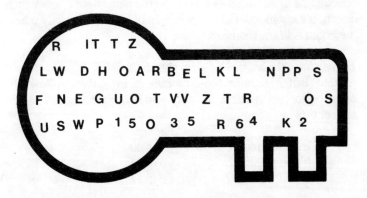

As you continue your trek through the fir trees, you chat to Miss Crumble about her spiritualism. 'Have you ever been in touch with anyone famous?' you ask with interest. 'Napoleon, for example?' Miss Crumble shakes her head honestly. 'Not Napoleon himself,' she admits, 'but I did once get in touch with Napoleon's dog. I could hear a distinct growling sound just after my glass had spelt out the letters of "Waterloo". It could only have been his dog!' You're not so certain about this, however. You don't recollect Napoleon having a dog. And as you glance down at Spooks, you notice there is a secret mischievous grin on his face! *Go to 20.*

The only window in the dark, poky nursery is a tiny oval one. Walking over to this window, Professor Bones wipes off some of the dust so he can peer through it. 'I can just make out a fountain outside,' he says. 'Let's look it up on the plan so we know which direction the window faces. It will help us work out exactly where this room is in the mansion.'

Do you have the estate PLAN in your FOLDER? If you do, use it to find which square the fountain is in – then follow the appropriate instruction. If not, you'll have to guess which instruction to follow.

If you think C1	go to 200
If you think C2	go to 34
If you think D2	go to 177

240

When you have recovered from this haunting, record it on the GHOST COUNTER. Now go to 149.

241

'Well, it hardly seems to matter that we can't open the box,' you console them both as you roll it over several times. 'I certainly can't *hear* anything inside it.' Just at the moment, the moon emerges from behind a cloud and you spot the huge dark shape of the mansion only a hundred metres to your right. 'Is it my short-sightedness,' the Professor asks with a shiver as he squints through his spectacles, 'or is there someone standing at the top of that tall tower?' You and Miss Crumble look in the direction that the Professor's shaking finger indicates, and focus on the tower . . . ***Go to 275.***

242

'What do we do now?' you ask, giving the padlock a frustrated tug. 'We've got to try and get into the stables somehow, just in case the diamonds are hidden inside.' It's then that you notice a small hole at the bottom of the stable door. It's much too small for you three to crawl through, but not for Spooks! 'Just go and have a quick sniff round, Spooks,' you plead with him. Very reluctantly, he finally obeys. But just as he's about to squeeze through the hole, you hear a rustling sound on the other side of the door. Is it the ghost of one of Sir Edward's horses? You all flee to a safe distance and then nervously look round to find out . . . *Go to 287.*

243

Miss Crumble is probably wishing that she hadn't suggested throwing the spirit dice after all because it decides that *she* should be the one to turn the well's handle! But she's totally fair about its decision and immediately rolls up her sleeves. With a horrible creaking noise, the handle slowly starts to move, winding up the rusty chain. The wooden bucket at the end finally comes to the surface . . . but alas, it's completely empty! Miss Crumble is just about to let the bucket down again, when you notice some numbers gouged into it. Could they be a date? Even more interesting are some roughly-carved symbols. Perhaps one of them is a clue!

Do you have SIR EDWARD'S WILL in your FOLDER? If you do, check whether any of the carved symbols shown below are included there – then follow the appropriate instruction to find out his clue. If you don't, go to 283 instead.

Sir Edward's clue tells you that the diamonds are not hidden anywhere in the grounds, but in the house itself! So you quickly leave the little graveyard and head back to the driveway. For a moment Spooks thinks you are going to the main gates and home . . . but Miss Crumble soon disappoints him. 'We're heading for the mansion now, Spooks,' she tells him enthusiastically. 'They'll probably be more ghosts there than you've had dog biscuits. Won't that be a treat?' Spooks nods his head dolefully. Yes, *what* a treat! **Go to 270.**

You could always try and force the door open, of course – but the chapel is holy and you don't really want to cause any damage. 'What do you think is behind the door, anyway?' you ask, curious. 'A little cupboard for storing hymn books or something?' Professor Bones tugs his little beard for a moment and then shakes his head. 'No, I think it was probably a priest's hole. In the old days people would squeeze in them to hide from their enemies.' You've all just turned away from this tiny door when you hear a faint moaning on the other side. Is it the ghost of one of those people who hid in there? Perhaps one who accidentally suffocated! You all rush to the other end of the chapel, sure that at any moment the locked door will fly open . . . **Go to 88.**

When you have recovered from this haunting, record it on the GHOST COUNTER. Now go to 15.

'It looks as if we just made it in time!' the Professor exclaims as there's a sudden crash of thunder outside. 'A storm has started!' You are really not sure which is worse, though; outside with the lightning . . . or inside this gloomy tower! When the Professor has lit one of his candles, you find that you are at the foot of an eerie spiral stairway, the stone steps disappearing into darkness. 'They must lead to the top of the tower,' Miss Crumble observes tensely. 'Since I'm sure there are no volunteers to be first up the stairway, I'll let my spirit dice decide who it's to be.'

Throw the SPIRIT DICE – then turn to the appropriate number.

If 💀 thrown   go to 98

If 🦇 thrown   go to 301

If 👻 thrown   go to 273

'W-w-who do you think that was?' you ask, trembling, as you all leap outside and slam the chapel door behind you. Professor Bones seems to know the answer but when he opens his mouth to tell you, nothing comes out. He's suffering from shock even more than you are! But then his sneezing returns, and with it his voice. 'I can't tell you his exact name,' he says, 'but he was a ghost of the classification *Ghostus Tormentus*. That's a very mischievous ghost. You can tell by that huge grin on his face.' Well, you certainly don't want to encounter that *Ghostus Tormentus* again and so you all agree to abandon the search of the chapel. You only hope the diamonds are somewhere else! **Go to 111.**

'The spirit dice has chosen *me* to take the lead, hasn't it, Miss Crumble?' you say, understanding the pained look she gives you. She nods her head. So, bracing yourself, you stride towards the stables, the others a short distance behind. The place is even spookier close to, your feet making horrible echoes on the cobbled exercise yard. As you're leading the way round the stables, you suddenly notice an old sundial above one of the doors. 'Look at those strange symbols on it,' you remark to the others. 'You don't think Sir Edward has hidden one of his clues there, do you?'

Do you have the WILL in your FOLDER? If you do, check whether any of the symbols shown below are included there –

then follow the appropriate instruction to find out Sir Edward's clue. If you don't have the WILL, go to 317 instead.

250

There is no point in becoming excited about the inscription. Since you don't have Sir Edward's will with you, there is no way of knowing whether there is one of his clues hidden in the illustration! As you're returning the book to the shelf, you suddenly hear a shuffling noise outside the door. It sounds as if someone is walking slowly along the hall! Then you think you hear china rattling on a tray. Is it the ghost of Sir Edward's maid, carrying a nightcap of cocoa to him? But you decide you're letting your imagination run away with you. The shuffling is probably just a draught, and the rattling china the hall candelabra quivering in this draught. So you bravely open the library door to peep outside . . . ***Go to 158.***

251

You're all greeted by a howling blast of wind as you finally reach the top of the tower and step out into the stormy night. 'Be careful of this little parapet,' you shout to the others after cautiously testing it. 'It's crumbling badly. I should keep well away from the edge!' But your time at the top of the tower is very brief because there's absolutely nothing up there – diamonds or anything else. As you climb back down the eerie stairway, you suddenly hear what sounds like a long cry from above. Is it just the wind, or is it the ghost of someone who tragically fell to their death from the tower? You all anxiously look back up to find out . . . ***Go to 50.***

When you have recovered from this haunting, record it on the GHOST COUNTER. Now go to 92.

Sir Edward's clue tells you that the diamonds are hidden in the top half of the house! 'That's really useful,' the Professor remarks enthusiastically. 'It saves us having to explore the kitchen and cellars. The cellars are normally the very worst place for ghosts.' The Professor suddenly remembers that the ghosts are meant to be the main reason he's here, though! 'Of course, it would be a great shame to miss any,' he adds hurriedly, going red. 'But the diamonds must be our priority!' ***Go to 47.***

You're just considering whether you should try and force the wardrobe open when your candle suddenly goes out! Was it a draught from the door that caused this, or did something *blow* it out? You anxiously ask Professor Bones for his opinion. 'Oh, a draught of course,' he replies rather uncertainly. 'An old house like this will have lots of draughts blowing through. Just light your candle again.' Taking the box of matches he passes to you, you nervously try to strike a light. You certainly can't see anything yet, but the room's still very dark. It will be a lot clearer in a second, when you've put the match to the candle . . . *Go to 170.*

'The spirit dice has decided that you should enter the chapel first, Professor Bones!' Miss Crumble tells him as she returns it to her pocket. 'Let's not waste any time, shall we?' So the Professor reluctantly marches up to the chapel's arched door but, on giving it a tug, he finds that it is firmly locked. 'It's odd that the spirit dice didn't warn us about that possibility,' the Professor remarks with a frown. 'Are you sure that it has these powers, Miss Crumble?' She starts to tremble with indignation and so you quickly interrupt before a row develops. 'Perhaps we should try one of those keys in the lock?' you suggest.

Do you have either of the KEYS in your FOLDER? If you do,

place it exactly over the chapel door's 'lock' below to see if it works – then follow the instruction. (You may try both KEYS if you have them.) If you don't have either of the KEYS – or your KEY doesn't work – go to 291 instead.

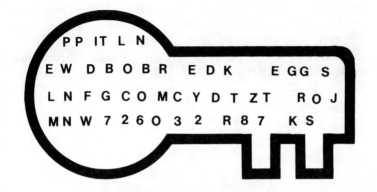

256

'The spirits have chosen *me* to lead again!' Miss Crumble announces weakly as she studies the roll of her dice. Lifting Spooks into her arms, she nervously starts to descend the crumbling steps. When you all finally reach the bottom, you find yourselves in an echoing stone chamber. There's an eerie dripping sound from somewhere. It seems that Professor Bones was right about it once being a dungeon. Suddenly your flickering candle lights up some rusty manacles dangling from the walls. Yes, he was definitely right! 'Perhaps we should try and locate this dungeon on the plan of the estate?' the Professor suggests in a tense whisper. 'We know that it's directly below the entrance to the tower. So we'll look *that* up.'

Do you have the PLAN in your FOLDER? If you do, use it to find which square the entrance to the tower is in – then follow the appropriate instruction. If not, you'll have to guess which instruction to follow.

If you think C3	go to 303
If you think B3	go to 197
If you think B2	go to 212

'Mr Creak!' you all exclaim with surprise and relief as he emerges from the shadows. 'What made *you* come to Ghostly Towers?' The old lawyer needs time to regain his breath before answering. And regain his nerves . . . for he's obviously had terrifying experiences getting here as well! 'To tell you the truth,' he begins, wiping his wrinkled brow, 'I almost wish I hadn't. The things I've seen in the grounds! But I thought I'd lend you a hand in your search for the diamonds. It can get a bit boring sitting in that dusty office of mine all day. For the first time in my life, I felt like a bit of an adventure!' *Go to 296.*

258

When you have recovered from this haunting, record it on the GHOST COUNTER. Now go to 22.

259

You just have to hope that there *wasn't* one of Sir Edward's clues hidden there, though – because you didn't bring his will with you! As you now turn away from the manacles to explore the rest of the eerie dungeon, you're sure you hear a slight rattling sound behind you. Every time *you* stop, *it* does too! 'It seems to be following us,' you remark in a petrified whisper. 'You don't think it's the skeleton of one of those prisoners who were manacled to the wall, do you?' You start to move again, and again you hear the rattling! There's only one thing for it. You're all going to have to look round and confront this persistent ghost . . . *Go to 279.*

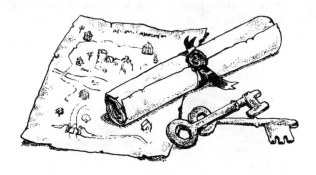

260

'Perhaps we'll have more luck with the other door,' Professor Bones says, and he immediately steps across to the one on the left and tries the handle. 'Yes, we do. This one's unlocked!' Cautiously entering the tiny dark room, you realise that it is a nursery. There's an old rocking-horse there, and toy soldiers scattered across the dusty floor. The Professor is just speculating whether the toy soldiers were Sir Edward's when you hear a creaking from the bottom of the wooden steps you just climbed. Is the sound just a delayed reaction from the rotten stairs, or is it caused by something standing on one of them? You all nervously creep back to the top of the stairway to check . . . *Go to 56.*

261

'You'd better give me the candle, Professor Bones,' Miss Crumble tells him after she has studied her spirit dice. 'It's *me* who is to lead up the staircase!' As you all follow her up the creaking stairs, you glance at the gloomy portraits on the wall. They're obviously the Oastley family. But as you pass the painting of Sir Giles Oastley, it strikes you as not being nearly as well-painted as all the others. In fact, you wonder whether Sir Edward jokingly did the painting himself, just to incorporate one of his clues! You ask Miss Crumble to bring her candle nearer the painting so you can have a better look.

Do you have the WILL in your FOLDER? If you do, check whether any detail in the painting below is included there – then follow the instruction to find out Sir Edward's clue. If you don't, go to 292 instead.

262

You don't have the estate plan with you, though. Anyway, you're sure this is just a ploy of the Professor's to put off passing through the gates. It's obvious where the gates would be on the plan – in the centre of the estate's boundary wall! Then the Professor seems to try another ploy, because he suddenly stops and asks if you heard something above. But then you hear it as well! Is this your first haunting, you wonder, feeling very nervous, as you all slowly lift your heads . . . *Go to 201.*

263

The Professor gives the gate a firm push in the hope that the lock might be very rusty and yield without a key. It doesn't, though. 'It looks as if we'll just have to walk all the way to the other end of the lake,' he says sadly. But Miss Crumble has other ideas. 'Nonsense, Professor!' she tells him. 'We can quite easily climb a little gate like this.' You're not so sure, though; if anyone slips while climbing the gate they could well fall off the bridge and into the water! You're just pointing this out to Miss Crumble when a white shape begins to emerge from the mist over the centre of the lake. It's coming towards you, growing bigger and bigger. You hope that it's just a swan . . . *Go to 120.*

264

Your trio has left the well far behind when it arrives at an odd-looking glass hut. At first you think it must be a greenhouse, but it's the wrong shape and there's a long wooden seat inside, running round the wall. 'It's a summer-house, my dear,' Miss Crumble explains. 'They were quite the rage in the old days. People would sit in them when the sun shone, to get nice and warm.' As you all step inside the summer-house to check if the diamonds are hidden there, you rather wish the sun would shine now. It's absolutely freezing! You don't find any diamonds, but you *do* find some funny little drawings. They've been carved into the seat, obviously a long time ago. 'They look like the handiwork of some mischievous child,' Professor Bones remarks. 'Perhaps of the young Sir Edward himself. I wonder, though, maybe he wasn't so young when he did them. It might be that he's cleverly hidden a clue here!'

Do you have the WILL in your FOLDER? If you do, check whether any of the drawings shown below are included there – then follow the appropriate instruction to find out Sir Edward's clue. If you don't, go to 16 instead.

265

Feeling very disappointed, your little group leaves the statue and continues up the driveway. You haven't walked very far, however, when Professor Bones suddenly stops dead in his tracks. He's sure he heard some laughter a short distance behind you. 'It could have just been a trick of the wind, I suppose,' he stammers. 'But I've got this awful feeling it's Sir Edward having a bit of a snigger at us all!' Well, there is only one way of confirming this. That is to turn round and check . . . *Go to 89.*

266

You suddenly remember that you don't have the plan of the estate with you, however. So you can't work out your exact location after all! Your little group has walked only a short way from the well, when you hear something which makes your blood run cold. It's a rusty, grinding noise. The well's handle seems to be turning of its own accord! 'Oh, it's nothing to worry about,' the Professor says as you all tentatively turn round to look. 'The weight of the bucket is just causing the chain to unwind again.' But then you see something certainly to worry about. For the handle suddenly starts to turn the other direction! The bucket is coming to the surface once more . . . *Go to 182.*

267

'It must be the ghost of Sir Edward's butler,' Professor Bones exclaims, all of a quiver. 'Who else would ask for our hat and cloak?' You hear no more of the voice but squeaky footsteps now start to approach from that direction! You all rush for the nearest door, desperately trying to open it so you can hide behind. But it's locked! You're going to have to find the right key, and *fast*!

Do you have either of the KEYS in your FOLDER? If you do,

place it exactly over the door's 'lock' below to see whether it works – then follow the instruction. (You may try both KEYS if you have them.) If you don't have either of the KEYS – or your KEY doesn't work – go to 102 instead.

268

You're just about to go and investigate the individual stables when you hear a snorting noise over to your right. It sounds like a horse, just returning from a brisk canter! You all quickly leave the stables and run and hide behind a tree some hundred metres away. Now there's the eerie sound of hooves on the cobbled exercise yard! Is it the ghost of one of Sir Edward's horses being led by the ghost of one of his stable lads? You all nervously peep from behind the tree to find out . . . *Go to 132.*

269

Although the ghost gives you a terrible fright, he also does you a favour. For he opens the locked door before suddenly fading away into nothingness. 'Some ghosts can be quite kind like that,' the Professor says knowingly, as if he hadn't really been that scared after all. 'Especially the unhappy-looking ones like him. They do their best to make sure others aren't equally miserable.' You all now step through the opened door and emerge into the fierce wind and rain. Climbing just a few more steps, you reach the very top of the tower. *Go to 278.*

Some fifteen minutes after leaving the chapel and its graveyard, your little group finds itself back on the driveway again. It's now quite dark and it's difficult to see more than fifty metres ahead. You're wondering why you didn't choose broad daylight to investigate the estate! 'What's that strange glow to the left?' you ask anxiously, but then you guess that it's just the moon reflecting on what must be a small lake. As the driveway takes you a little nearer to the eerie glow, you see that there is indeed an expanse of water there, and a little boathouse at the edge. You suggest locating it on the plan of the estate so you'll have a rough idea how far up the driveway you are.

Do you have the PLAN in your FOLDER? If you do, use it to find which square the boathouse is in – then follow the appropriate instruction. If not, you'll have to guess which instruction to follow.

If you think C2	go to 121
If you think C3	go to 96
If you think D3	go to 8

Since you don't have Sir Edward's will with you, though, you obviously won't be able to interpret the clue – even if there is one hidden there! So your little group leaves the top of the tower and returns down the dark stairway. You haven't descended very far, however, when you hear what sounds like someone calling out at the top! 'Perhaps it's Sir Edward's ghost?' Miss Crumble suggests. 'Maybe he's spotted Lady Rowena in the gardens below and is calling out his love to her!' But then you hear a flapping sound. It must just be an owl. But you decide to return to the top to put your minds at rest. Is it an owl or isn't it, you wonder with breath held, as you approach the last step . . . *Go to 173.*

Feeling very disappointed, you get to your feet again and are just about to step round the chest when Miss Crumble suddenly presses a finger to her mouth. 'Ssh!' she orders anxiously. 'I'm sure I heard a shuffling noise downstairs!' To begin with you think it's just Spooks trying to escape out of the front door, for he's no longer at your feet. But then you spot him cowering behind the chest. So what's that shuffling round downstairs? Did Miss Crumble just imagine it, or is it a ghost? You all tensely lean over the banisters to try and find out . . . *Go to 209.*

Miss Crumble gravely studies the roll of her spirit dice, then slowly raises her plump face towards . . . *you*! So with a shaking hand you take the candle from the Professor and start to climb the eerie stairway. 'Be very careful,' you warn the others over your shoulder. 'A lot of these steps are crumbling away.' You haven't climbed much further when you suddenly freeze. There's a clonking noise coming down the steps! It sounds like someone dragging a ball and chain. You all immediately race back to the oak door at the bottom of the tower. When you reach it, however, you find that it is now mysteriously locked! It's going to need a key, and *fast*!

Do you have either of the KEYS in your FOLDER? If you do, place it exactly over the door's 'lock' below to see whether it works – then follow the instruction. (You may try both KEYS if you have them.) If you don't have either of the KEYS – or your KEY doesn't work – go to 164 instead.

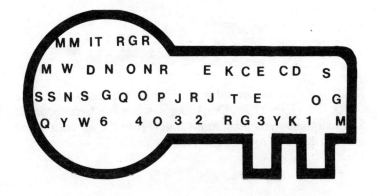

Convinced that the box *is* a coffin, you're very relieved that the Professor is unable to unlock it. What if there's a skeleton inside! But, on the other hand, what if the diamonds are in there? It would be a pity to have come all this way and then give up only centimetres away from the jewels. You wonder whether you should try and *force*

the box open. Suddenly, though, there's a rattling from inside it!
Has a mouse somehow found its way in, or were you right about the
skeleton? You all rush to the other end of the dungeon and then peer
through your trembling fingers at the box . . . **Go to 315.**

When you have recovered from this haunting, record it on the
GHOST COUNTER. (Don't forget: when you have recorded
four hauntings, you must immediately stop the adventure and
start the game all over again.) Now go to 140.

'What a pity we didn't bring Sir Edward's will with us,' Professor
Bones remarks. 'I'm sure there *is* one of his clues there on the
window. I can just see the old devil licking his finger and playfully
drawing in the dust!' You're all just about to turn away from the little
window when something very strange happens. The drawings
suddenly start to disappear! 'Perhaps it is just our breath blowing
the dust away,' you suggest, not feeling very hopeful . . . but then

there's a creaking noise from the bottom of the stairway you just climbed. Has Sir Edward come back to tease you? You all anxiously creep back to the top of the stairs to take a look . . . ***Go to 56.***

Go to 56.

277

'What a shame we don't have Sir Edward's will with us,' Miss Crumble adds disappointedly. 'I'd bet my favourite crystal ball there's a clue hidden here!' She's hardly finished her sentence when you hear a strange moaning sound from underneath the bridge. 'It's probably just the wind whistling through,' she says, trying to be reassuring as you all run some way from the bridge, not daring to look round. But you and Professor Bones eventually decide she must be right. After all, the surface of the lake is rippling quite a bit. So you now all slowly turn your eyes back towards the bridge . . . ***Go to 175.***

278

'I hope the lightning holds off for a while,' Professor Bones remarks anxiously as you start to look around the top of the tower. 'We're very vulnerable up here with it being the highest point of the mansion. One quick flash and we could be burnt to a cinder!' You really wish Professor Bones wouldn't alarm you like this. As if you haven't got enough to worry about with all the ghosts! But, fortunately, your stay at the top of the tower looks like being a very short one. There's absolutely nothing up there! Returning to the door, however, you notice there are some doodles carved into it. You wonder if one of these is a clue from Sir Edward.

Do you have the WILL in your FOLDER? If you do, check whether any of the doodles shown below are included there – then follow the instruction to find out Sir Edward's clue. If you don't have the WILL, go to 298 instead.

But when you all turn your heads, you find that there is nothing there! Either the ghost has disappeared, or you just imagined the rattling sound. So you start moving once more. *Oh no!* The rattling has suddenly returned! You all swing round much more quickly this time . . . but again there's only empty air behind you. It's then that you notice Miss Crumble's necklace. 'I think I've found our skeleton, Miss Crumble,' you chuckle with relief. 'It's those long, dangly beads of yours!' Your theory is confirmed when you ask her to walk a few more steps. The beads merrily rattle away as she does so! *Go to 212.*

Now for the moment of truth. Professor Bones has been able to find the way into the centre of the maze, but will he be able to find the way out again? 'As I say, it's just a matter of applying a few basic geometric principles,' he says as he leads you left and right. After a good fifteen minutes of the Professor applying these basic geometric principles, however, you find yourselves back at the centre of the maze again! 'Oh really, Professor Bones!' Miss Crumble says, tutting impatiently. 'I think we'll let Spooks show us the way out this time. All he has to do is pick up our scent.' *Go to 122.*

When you have recovered from this haunting, record it on the GHOST COUNTER. Now go to 22.

You've heard of absent-minded professors, but this is ridiculous! It was just minutes ago that you told Professor Bones that you unfortunately didn't bring Sir Edward's will with you. 'Of course you did!' the Professor now remembers, scratching his domed head. 'It was at the gate, wasn't it? Silly old me!' You're just about to continue up the driveway when Spooks suddenly runs off into the trees to the right. 'He must have sensed a spirit ahead,' Miss Crumble explains as you all chase after him, worried that he might get lost. 'He's very sensitive that way!' You at last catch up with him, but it's not just Spooks who's lost now, it's all four of you. The trees are quite thick and dark, almost like a wood. Even worse, you suddenly spot a strange white mist ahead. Is it forming into a ghost? *Go to 126.*

283

Without Sir Edward's will, however, there's no way of telling if there's a clue hidden on the bucket. So your little group leaves the well and continues its exploration of the grounds. But you've only walked twenty metres or so when you hear a series of loud noises echoing behind you. They're coming from the bottom of the well! 'It must be Spooks!' Miss Crumble cries out, suddenly noticing that her little dog is missing. 'He's fallen in!' Frantic, you all run back to the well, and lean over the edge. As you're peering down into the dark hole, however, there's a little bark at your ankles. It's Spooks! But if it's not him in that darkness down the well, who – or what – is it . . . ? *Go to 25.*

'It looks like a huge jack-in-the-box,' Miss Crumble says, fascinated, as she studies the brightly-coloured box. 'They were very popular in Sir Edward's time. You open the lid and out jumps a naughty jack!' Of course, you're all wondering if there might be something in the box in addition to the surprise toy. The diamonds! To find out, though, you are going to have to produce the right key because there is a large lock holding down the box's lid!

Do you have either of the KEYS in your FOLDER? If you do, place it exactly over the box's 'lock' below to see whether it works – then follow the instruction. (You may try both KEYS if you have them.) If you don't have either of the KEYS – or your KEY doesn't work – go to 131 instead.

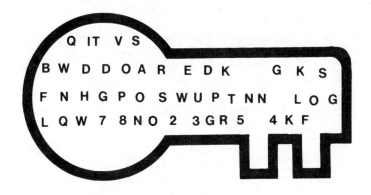

The next door you come to on the ground floor of the house opens on to a small room with a piano. It must be the music room! The piano is riddled with woodworm and is so badly decayed that Miss Crumble can't get a single note out of it. 'What a shame!' she says with a sigh. 'I'm such a beautiful pianist aren't I, Spooks? Sometimes he loves my playing so much that when I have to stop for one of my seances he starts to growl!' While you're listening to Miss Crumble, the Professor strolls over to the cracked window. He seems to be waiting for another flash of lightning. 'I can just see a weeping willow out there,' he says when it comes, illuminating the sky. 'If we locate it on the plan of the estate, it will enable us to work out which direction this window faces.'

Do you have the PLAN in your FOLDER? If you do, use it to find which square the weeping willow is in – then follow the appropriate instruction. If not, you'll have to guess which instruction to follow.

If you think B3	go to 106
If you think C3	go to 213
If you think C2	go to 125

286

You all try and think of another way of getting inside the bucket. The Professor scratches his domed head, Spooks scratches the back of his ear, and Miss Crumble closes her eyes in the hope of getting one of her messages from beyond. 'I think something's coming!' she announces in a strange sort of chant, as she slowly sways her head. 'Who's there? Can you help us open the bucket? Reveal yourself!' You and Professor Bones suddenly look up as there's a movement amongst the trees about thirty metres to your left. Something is disturbing the fallen leaves there. It appears that Miss Crumble's call on the spirits has worked! You only hope that it is the right sort of spirit . . . **Go to 7.**

***When you have recovered from this haunting, record it on the
GHOST COUNTER. Now go to 176.***

288

You enter the dovecot to give it a quick search, scaring away all the
birds at the top as you do so. All except one, that is. For you can still
hear a cooing up there. 'I wonder why it wasn't frightened off like all
the others?' you ask, curious. But then you begin to wonder
whether it is a dove at all. The cooing grows louder and louder,
much too loud for any bird. 'Quick, let's get out of here!' you cry. 'I
think it might be a ghost!' When you're all safely outside, you slowly
look towards the top of the dovecot to see if anything has squeezed
out of one of the holes . . . ***Go to 32.***

289

When you finally reach the bottom of the spiral stairway again, you
decide that you've spent more than enough time in the tower now.
Either the diamonds are hidden somewhere else in the mansion . . .
or, if they *were* hidden here, they've since been removed. For you

couldn't have made a more thorough search of this eerie annexe. Or could you? Just as you're about to leave the tower, Spooks starts sniffing at the stone floor. 'Look, there's a badly-fitting stone slab down here!' you exclaim as you brush away the dust with your feet. There must be more to the tower – *underground*!' You're all wondering how you can raise the heavy stone, when Professor Bones kicks something as he is brushing away some more of the thick dust. It's a trap-door, and there's a large ring embedded in it! *Go to 27.*

290

'The spirits have decided that *you* should run ahead, my dear,' Miss Crumble tells you as she studies her dice. Well, you won't argue with the dice's decision, but you're certainly not going to *run* towards the shadowy figure. You'll approach very slowly! When you eventually reach the figure, however, you find that Professor Bones was right about it being just a statue in a fountain. 'Look at this,' you say to the others as they now join you. 'There's a tiny locked door at the base of the fountain. I wonder if one of those keys would open it?'

Do you have either of the KEYS in your FOLDER? If you do, place it exactly over the tiny door's 'lock' below to see if it works – then follow the instruction. (You may try both KEYS if you have them.) If you don't have either of the KEYS – or your KEY doesn't work – go to 309 instead.

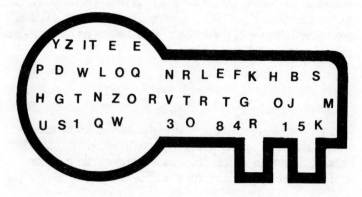

You're just thinking that you're going to have to forget about entering the chapel when you hear an excited bark from round the other side. It's Spooks, and he's found another little door! You're all delighted to find that this one isn't locked . . . or are you? For horrible cobwebs trail across your face as you enter the gloomy interior, and the atmosphere here is cold and eerie. You hope this search isn't going to take long! You've scarcely started looking under the dusty pews, however, when you're given a terrible fright. The door suddenly slams shut again! Was it just a gust of wind that caused this or a mischievous ghost? You all hurry to one of the broken windows to see if there's anything lurking outside . . . *Go to 246.*

Well, maybe there is one of Sir Edward's clues hidden in the portrait, maybe there isn't . . . but since you don't have his will, you'll never know! You therefore continue up the creaking staircase, approaching the shadowy landing at the top. You've just reached this landing, wondering whether to explore the rooms to left or right, when you all nearly jump out of your skins. Behind you, one of those paintings suddenly drops from the wall, crashing all the way down to the bottom of the staircase. You're sure it was the one you were just looking at! Either you wobbled it a little, or Sir Giles Oastley has suddenly come to life. You all slowly turn your heads to find out which . . . *Go to 304.*

**When you have recovered from this haunting, record it on the
GHOST COUNTER. Now go to 39.**

294

Having quickly searched the little bedroom, you now decide to
leave it to explore some of the others. You hope you'll have more
luck with one of these! Just as Miss Crumble is shutting the door
behind you, however, you hear the shattering of glass in the room. It
must be the window-pane! Your first thought is a violent ghost, but
Professor Bones says there could be a more rational explanation for
the window breaking. The fierce wind, for instance, or the thunder
vibrations. Finally persuaded by this, you all peep round the
door . . . *Go to 228.*

295

You're just about to remind the Professor that you chose not to bring
Sir Edward's will with you when you notice something odd about
the curtains. They're twitching! Miss Crumble is convinced that
this is evidence of a spirit in the drawing-room, and she is about to go
off into one of her trances. But the Professor says it's probably just a

draught from the windows. 'If you don't mind me saying so, Miss Crumble,' he gently chides her, 'you're letting the atmosphere of this place get to you a little. Now, if you draw back the curtains, I'm sure you'll find that one of the windows just isn't closed properly.' As he's so confident, though, Miss Crumble invites him to do it! His face suddenly changing colour, he slowly approaches the curtains and yanks them back . . . *Go to 328.*

296

You all examine the tall racks of wine bottles along the walls of the cellar. Could the diamonds be inside one of those bottles? 'See if any of their corks have been tampered with,' Professor Bones suggests eagerly. But checking every single one of the dusty bottles is going to take days. There are hundreds of them, row upon row! You're just scanning the very bottom row, however, when you spot a large sheet of card lying there. 'Look, it's the menu for one of Sir Edward's banquets!' you exclaim as you pick it up and read out some of the exotic courses listed there. 'Roast venison and pheasant Oastley-style. The cook must have left it here when she came to fetch some more wine.' You then begin to wonder about the decoration round the edge of the menu. Could it possibly hide one of Sir Edward's clues?

Do you have the WILL in your FOLDER? If you do, check

whether any part of the decoration shown below is included there – then follow the appropriate instruction to find out Sir Edward's clue. If not, go to 321 instead.

Menu

Grouse pâté
*
Pheasant, Oastley style
Roast Venison
*
Brandy truffles
*
Cheese

297

'Well, never mind,' you console Professor Bones about the locked shutter. 'I'm sure the diamonds wouldn't have been hidden behind there, anyway. An open ledge would have been much too risky a place for them. You forget that there are ravens nesting around this tower. They're often attracted to sparkly things and can fly off with them!' In fact, that sounds like a raven now, further up the stairway. It must have flown in from the top. But isn't the top closed off by a locked door? So perhaps it's not a raven at all . . . *Go to 110.*

298

'What a pity we don't have Sir Edward's will with us!' Miss Crumble sighs disappointedly. You're all just about to pass through the door to return to the bottom of the tower when there's a loud shrieking sound from the stormy darkness above you. 'Don't be alarmed,' the Professor says to reassure you. 'I expect it's just bats shrieking. They won't do us any harm. They're really quite friendly creatures!' But you're not so certain that it is just bats – surely they have a very high-pitched cry? And what are those two bright green things that are coming towards you now, out of the darkness? They look like large eyes! ***Go to 108.***

299

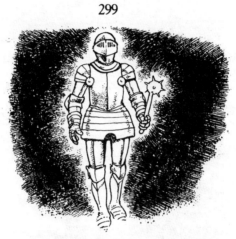

When you have recovered from this haunting, record it on the GHOST COUNTER. Now go to 205.

300

'Ah!' Miss Crumble exclaims as she studies the face of the dice. 'I'm afraid the spirits have decided that you should be the one to try the gates, Professor Bones!' Turning even whiter than he was before, the Professor nonetheless graciously accepts the decision of the dice and puts a skinny hand to the large iron ring. With much creaking, it turns! 'Before we go any further,' the Professor suddenly says, 'perhaps we should locate these gates on the plan of the estate. It will help us get our bearings.'

Do you have the PLAN of the estate in your FOLDER? If you do, use it to find which square the main gates are in – then follow

the appropriate instruction below. If you don't have the PLAN in your FOLDER, you'll have to guess which instruction to follow.

If you think B4	go to 58
If you think C4	go to 112
If you think D4	go to 262

301

'Come on, Spooks!' Miss Crumble says, picking up her little dog after she has studied her spirit dice. 'The spirits have decided that *we* should lead up the steps!' Spooks doesn't seem very happy about this, though, sure that the dice had only specified Miss Crumble! But she carries him round and round the shadowy stairway, up and up, and finally brings you all to a small wooden door right at the top. She's just trying the door when you hear a clonking noise from further down the steps . . . ***Go to 192.***

302

'Come on then, follow me!' Miss Crumble says jauntily, after the spirit dice has apparently decided that she should lead the way towards the lake. As the mist-shrouded lake comes nearer and nearer, however, her pace grows slower and slower. 'This must have been the boathouse,' you whisper as you finally reach a delapidated wooden hut at the water's edge. 'You don't think the diamonds are hidden inside, do you?' When you investigate the flimsy door at the back of the boathouse, however, you find that it is secured by a large padlock. 'Perhaps it can be unlocked by one of those two large keys?' the Professor suggests.

Do you have either of the KEYS in your FOLDER? If you have, place it exactly over the 'lock' below to see if it works – then follow the instruction. (You may try both keys if you have them.) If you don't have either of the KEYS – or your KEY doesn't work – go to 216 instead.

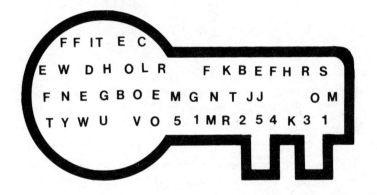

303

Your little group now begins its search of the dark, echoing chamber. Spooks is hoping that he'll be able to remain in his mistress's arms, but she gently lowers him to the damp stone floor. 'There you are, Spooks!' she says, patting him on the head. 'I know that you don't like being carried but I was worried about those steep, slippery steps!' You keep as far away from the eerie manacles as possible while exploring the dungeon, scared that they might start to rattle. It's a good job you have kept your distance – because suddenly you hear a clanking of iron! Hoping that this was merely caused by the draught from the trap-door above, you all nervously take another peep at the manacles . . . *Go to 222.*

When you have recovered from this haunting, record it on the GHOST COUNTER. Now go to 47.

305

You were perhaps expecting to see a bleeding, severed head floating in the middle of the room. But, to your huge relief, this isn't the cause of the dripping at all. It's not blood that's dripping, but rainwater! 'There must be some tiles missing on the roof above this room,' the Professor says. 'When there's a bad storm like now, the rain obviously seeps through.' He takes on that learned look of his again, tugging at his wispy beard. 'You see, you must always think of the logical explanations first. It really doesn't pay to jump to conclusions!' The funny thing is that the Professor jumped to the conclusion about the blood before any of you! *Go to 199.*

306

A troubled look on Miss Crumble's face tells you that it is *she* whom the spirit dice has decided on to lead up the staircase. The wooden steps seem to grow narrower and narrower, creakier and creakier, as you, Professor Bones and Spooks tentatively follow her towards the top. There's a small, shadowy landing there, with doors to left and right. Entering the left door, you find yourselves in what was obviously once the nursery. There's an old rocking-horse in the middle, draped with heavy cobwebs, and toy soldiers scattered across the dusty floor. *Go to 239.*

307

Miss Crumble gives you a sympathetic look after she has glanced at her spirit dice. 'I'm afraid it's decided on you again, my dear!' she says. You're beginning to wonder how honest her interpretation of the dice is, but you cautiously advance towards the dark figure. 'You're right, Miss Crumble!' you call back with relief. 'It is just a statue. A statue of one of Sir Edward's ancestors!' As you all gather round it, commenting on how eccentric the ancestor looked, the Professor notices a crest at the base of the statue. 'Another one!' he remarks thoughtfully. 'And a different type too. I wonder if *this* hides a clue from Sir Edward? Let's have a look at his will.'

Do you have SIR EDWARD'S WILL in your FOLDER? If you do, check whether any part of the crest below is included there – then follow the appropriate instruction to find out his clue. If you don't, go to 282 instead.

You've walked only a few metres on from the garden seat when Miss Crumble suddenly stops dead in her tracks. Her arms float out in front of her, the fingers quivering. She seems to be going into one of her trances. 'Is there something you want to tell me?' she moans, her eyes closed. 'I'm listening. Speak! Speak!' When her eyes have at last opened again, you wonder if this strange experience might have been upsetting for her. But she seems perfectly cheerful about it. 'I've just had a message from beyond,' she tells you brightly. 'We're to leave this driveway and explore over to the right.' *Go to 20.*

'Never mind,' says Professor Bones, when you find that you're unable to unlock the tiny door. 'It's probably just to give access to the workings of the fountain in case it breaks down. I doubt very much that the diamonds are hidden in there.' You're just about to return to the driveway when you hear what sounds like a woman's happy laughter coming from that direction. It grows louder and louder. 'You don't think it's the ghost of Rowena coming to sit by the fountain?' you ask, trembling. Well, none of you is waiting to find out and you all race off towards the right, only stopping when you're a good two hundred metres from the fountain. You now slowly turn your heads to see if you were right about the ghost of Lady Rowena . . . *Go to 240.*

When you have recovered from this haunting, record it on the
GHOST COUNTER. Now go to 269.

'But you know jolly well that we don't have the estate plan with us,'
Miss Crumble says, wagging her finger at you, guessing your game.
'Now, where was I? Oh yes, the weeping lady at Berkley Manor.
Legend has it that . . .' But Miss Crumble's story suddenly ends in
a piercing scream. 'What's that sound behind us?' she asks shakily.
'It's coming from the middle of the lake. I am sure it's someone
weeping!' Hoping that it's just her vivid imagination, you all
apprehensively glance back towards the lake . . . ***Go to 74.***

As it turns out, it doesn't matter that you can't unlock the door because you suddenly notice that one of the panes of glass at the back of the summer-house is missing. You can just step in without using the door! Unfortunately, your luck doesn't continue . . . because a quick search of the interior reveals neither diamonds, nor even a clue. 'We'd better get moving again,' you remark. 'Look, it's growing darker by the minute.' As you're staring out at the fading dusk, something taps the glass behind you. Tensely turning round, you all pray that it was just the branch of a tree . . . ***Go to 258.***

After quickly leaving the stables, you're surprised several minutes later to come across a very old four-wheeled coach. 'What's that doing here, in the middle of nowhere?' you ask suspiciously. 'Surely its proper place is back where the horses were kept.' You start to wonder about the coach: is it just a ghostly apparition? But while you're wondering, Spooks bravely trots up to it, stands up on his hind legs, and leans against one of the back wheels. It is real after all. You, Miss Crumble and the Professor now start to examine the rusty coach yourselves, wondering if the diamonds might be hidden inside. But when you try to open the door, you find that it is locked. Perhaps one of those two keys will do the trick?

Do you have either of the KEYS in your FOLDER? If you do,

*place it exactly over the 'lock' below – then follow the instruction.
(You may try both KEYS if you have them.) If you don't have
either of the KEYS – or your KEY doesn't work – go to 162
instead.*

314

Since you don't have the plan of the estate with you, however,
there's no way of confirming whether it's a summer-house.
Anyway, you now enter the little glass building, just in case it *is* the
diamonds' hiding place. While you're all searching the dusty floor,
you suddenly hear a tapping sound above you. 'Perhaps an owl has
landed on the roof,' the Professor says, his teeth chattering. 'Do you
think we ought to look up and check?' You and Miss Crumble are as
reluctant as he is, though, and you keep your eyes nervously
downwards. And Spooks has his eyes completely covered with his
paws! 'Oh, this is ridiculous!' Miss Crumble remarks. 'When I
count to three, we'll all look up. One . . . two . . . three!' *Go to 81.*

When you have recovered from this haunting, record it on the GHOST COUNTER. Now go to 212.

316

You're just about to venture into the dovecot when you think you hear chuckling from inside. Could it be a ghost? 'Of course it isn't, dear,' Miss Crumble says. 'It's just the doves. I know because I used to keep them myself. They make this purring sound in their throats.' But then the chuckle changes to something more like a cackle. Surely doves don't make that sort of sound as well? Miss Crumble is inclined to agree with you this time and so you all nervously retreat from the dovecot. When you're a good hundred metres back, you slowly look up towards the top of the little building. That cackle has now changed to a horrible wail! *Go to 32.*

317

In your excitement about the symbols, you'd forgotten that you had, of course, chosen not to bring Sir Edward's will with you! You and Miss Crumble have just turned away from the sundial when the

Professor lets out a sudden gasp. 'Haven't you noticed something odd?' he asks. 'Look, there's a shadow thrown by the sundial and yet there isn't any sun. Hardly any light at all, in fact.' A few seconds later, you all observe something even odder. The shadow begins to race round the dial, like the hand of a clock gone beserk! 'It must be caused by something just above our heads,' the Professor exclaims, nervously starting to look up. 'Something very bright and mischievous . . .' *Go to 95.*

318

Miss Crumble looks as if she wishes she hadn't suggested using the spirit dice again so quickly, after all. For it decides that *she* should now lead. But she bravely takes the Professor's candle from him and ventures into the eerie house. She leads you through a panelled hall, her candle making flickering shadows on the dark wood, and then towards the first door. 'It's the library!' she whispers as she cautiously pushes the door open and enters a dusty room full of leather-bound books. The shelves run all the way across three walls, from floor to ceiling. 'The whole collection must be worth a fortune!' the Professor remarks as he takes one of the books out and delicately turns the pages. *Go to 185.*

319

'Me again,' Miss Crumble mutters disappointedly as she interprets the roll of her dice. 'Oh well, I can't argue with the will of the spirits!' So she immediately hurries towards the shadowy figure, her clumsy feet nearly tripping her up once or twice. 'Nothing to worry about, everybody,' she calls back a few minutes later. 'It *is* just a statue in a fountain. A charming maid pouring a jug.' As you join Miss Crumble at the fountain, she draws your attention to some symbols carved into the rim of the now-empty pool. 'I wonder if one of these is a clue from Sir Edward?' she asks thoughtfully, toying with the large beads that dangle from her neck. 'I reckon there's a fair chance!'

Do you have the WILL in your FOLDER? If you do, use it to check whether any of the symbols shown below are included there – then follow the instruction to find out Sir Edward's clue. If you don't, go to 113.

320

You're all terrified that the skeleton is going to break loose from its manacles and stroll over to you. But, to your immense relief, it waves a little bony goodbye and then fades away into nothingness. The manacles are empty again! You, Miss Crumble and Spooks now search one side of the dungeon while Professor Bones searches another. 'I hope we don't find any torture instruments . . .' you remark with a shiver as you both edge along. Suddenly, that skeleton appears again right behind you, tapping Miss Crumble on the shoulder! 'Oh, it's just you, Professor!' she exclaims with relief after focusing her eyes. 'I do wish you would put on some weight!' *Go to 212.*

321

Since you don't have Sir Edward's will with you, however, you disappointedly drop the menu. But, as it falls to the stone floor, you notice that there's some more writing on the back. Is this just additional courses for the meal, or is it an instruction from Sir Edward? It proves to be the latter, but not the sort of instruction you were hoping for, about the diamonds. Sir Edward warns you to *leave* Ghostly Towers this very second, or your sanity will be at risk! You daren't ignore his warning, and so you all hurriedly make your way back to the mansion's front door and then up the driveway towards the gates. You'll just have to return to the mansion some other time, when your nerves are a lot stronger!

Your exploration of Ghostly Towers wasn't a success on this occasion. If you would like another attempt, you must start the game again from the beginning. Try setting off with a different ITEM next time to see if it gives you more luck.

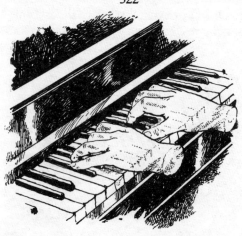

When you have recovered from this haunting, record it on the GHOST COUNTER. Now go to 178.

323

'Well, Miss Crumble?' the Professor asks excitedly when she has used the key to unlock the iron box. 'Are the diamonds inside or not?' She shakes her head disappointedly. 'I'm afraid they're not, Professor Bones,' she replies. 'But there is *something* tucked away at the bottom. It appears to be another copy of Sir Edward's will. He must have hidden it here in case his lawyers lost the original.'

If you don't already have it there, put the WILL into the slit of your FOLDER. Now go to 101.

324

Pushing open the rusty gate, you all enter the overgrown maze. 'Is this wise do you think, Miss Crumble?' you ask, having second thoughts as you glance up at the darkening sky. 'If we get lost inside, it might well be pitch black before we find our way out again.' But Professor Bones assures you that you won't get lost. 'Finding one's way through a maze is simply a matter of applying a few basic geometric principles,' he informs you pompously. 'To a professor like myself, it should be a piece of cake.' Well, he certainly manages to find the middle of the maze all right. There's a little garden seat there and, under the seat, a small flat tin. Are the diamonds inside? Unfortunately, no . . . but there is a plan of the estate!

If you don't already have it there, put the PLAN into your FOLDER. Now go to 280.

325

'Well, suits of armour have sometimes been known to come to life,' the Professor says, defending himself rather coyly as he continues to lead you through the hall. 'I heard of a case once when a suit of armour was found the next morning sitting at the breakfast table, having a nice cup of tea!' This is a story that even Spooks doesn't seem to believe, however, cocking a dubious ear! You all follow the Professor towards a wide double door on the right. 'This must be the banqueting room, where the Oastleys did all their entertaining,' he guesses. When he tries to open the doors, however, he finds that they are firmly locked. 'I wonder if this is what one of those keys is for?' he asks.

Do you have either of the KEYS in your FOLDER? If you do,

place it exactly over the door's 'lock' below to see whether it works – then follow the instruction. (You may try both KEYS if you have them.) If you don't have either of the KEYS – or your KEY doesn't work – go to 211 instead.

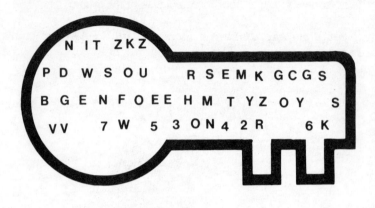

326

Having pushed the stable door open, you all quickly search inside. 'That's odd,' the Professor remarks. 'This straw seems quite fresh and yet these stables are meant to have been abandoned a long time ago. Perhaps there's a ghost horse that uses them!' You really wish the Professor would keep such thoughts to himself and you quicken your search of the straw, wanting to leave this eerie place as soon as possible. When Miss Crumble suddenly lets out a loud cry, you think your wish has been granted. Has she discovered the diamonds under the straw? No . . . just a mouse! ***Go to 176.***

After entering the summer-house, you immediately stamp around its dusty floor to see if there are any loose floorboards. 'Here's one!' the Professor suddenly exclaims with excitement. But when he prises it up to investigate underneath he finds just an empty hole there. Well, not completely empty, because a brown toad suddenly jumps out, making the Professor leap into the air with fright. 'It won't do you any harm, Professor,' you say to reassure him, although you're again having a few doubts about your learned companion. If he's like this with a little toad, what's he going to be like with a full-size ghost! *Go to 22.*

When you have recovered from this haunting, record it on the GHOST COUNTER. Now go to 178.

'What are we going to do?' Professor Bones asks with alarm after all your attempts to try and force the door open have failed. 'We could be trapped down here for ever!' But as you give the door just one final heave with your shoulders, it suddenly comes free. It has mysteriously unlocked itself again! 'Well, I just don't understand it,' Professor Bones remarks as you all now quickly climb out of the dungeon. 'Presumably, though, this is the work of some ghosts. They're obviously trying to persuade us to leave the mansion.' So this is exactly what you will do . . . *immediately*, before the ghosts plan something a lot more serious for you!

Your exploration of Ghostly Towers wasn't a success on this occasion. If you would like another attempt, you must start the game again from the beginning. Try setting out with a different ITEM next time to see if it gives you more luck.

330

When you have recovered from this haunting, record it on the GHOST COUNTER. Now go to 270.

331

You at last reach the end of the dark, eerie stairway and step out into the howling wind at the very top of the tower. There's absolutely nothing up here, though – diamonds or anything else! You're just thinking what a waste of time the long climb up the stairway was (not to mention the strain on the nerves) when Professor Bones starts to investigate the little parapet's stonework. 'Come and have a look at these strange carvings here,' he says. 'One of them could possibly be a clue from Sir Edward!'

Do you have the WILL in your FOLDER? If you do, check whether any of the carvings shown below are included there – then follow the appropriate instruction to find out Sir Edward's clue. If not, go to 271 instead.

332
Hurrying right round to the back of the mansion, you finally spot another door. It's at the bottom of a large round tower attached to the house. 'I hope this one doesn't have something behind it as well!' Miss Crumble remarks as she grips the handle on the heavy oak door. To begin with, it seems that it does. But when you and the Professor give Miss Crumble your assistance, the door slowly starts to creak open. It's now just about wide enough for you all to squeeze inside the cold, dark tower! *Go to 247.*